COAST WALKS

One Hundred Adventures
Along the California Coast

John McKinney

Olympus Press

SANTA BARBARA, CALIFORNIA

CONTENTS

Central Coast

North Coast

"As the last sight and sound of people faded away, the trail narrowed, my own kind of trees and free wild places closed around me. The headlands stood black against the last sun-glow over the ocean, and the quiet mountains waiting to be climbed seemed to fold on and on forever..."

—*Lillian Bos Ross*
The Stranger: A Novel of Big Sur

Foreword

Other states have snowy peaks, wild rivers and vast deserts, but only California has a coastline of such length and diversity. This is a book about walking that coastline, from the Mexican border to the Oregon border, an invitation to walk along land's end for one mile or ten, a chance to experience what many consider to be the greatest meeting of land and sea in the world.

This book describes coast walks—around precious wetlands, along precipitous bluffs, across white sand beaches, around bays, across islands, to lighthouses, and through redwood forests. In this guide, the walker will find days, weekends, and weeks of exploration and recreation along one of the most unique environments on earth.

Walks in this guide explore dozens of state beaches, marine refuges, and reserves. Other walks climb inland through the chaparral-cloaked Santa Monica and Santa Ynez Mountains, through the Santa Lucia Mountains of Big Sur, over the Santa Cruz Mountains, the hills around San Francisco Bay, the precipitous King Range of Humboldt County.

There are outings in this guide for walkers of every age and ability. Easy "leg stretchers" are the perfect antidote to the sometimes frustrating drive along the Coast Highway. Many trails are suitable for families with small children. And serious hikers will find a number of challenging routes.

Lastly, and perhaps most importantly, this book is about the California coastline, its sand strands and cobble shores, its fists of mountains rising above the surf, its tides and tidepools, its past, its present, its future.

By seeing the many "coasts" of California, you begin to understand the whole. The more you hike, the more various are the habitats you encounter, and the more you realize how interdependent they are. These habitats are links in a single chain, dependent on mankind for their continued survival.

What coast walking provides is a microview of the coastline, a slow-motion study of land and sea, a link between ourselves and the edge of the continent.

May the chain remain unbroken.

-J.M.

Coast Walking to a New Land Ethic

If, with a wave of a wand, one could magically link together the 800 or so miles of coastal trail described in this book, the result would be a splendorous California Coastal Trail. This trail would be an urban-rural-wilderness collage—the best of far western civilization, plus the best of what has remained untouched by far western civilization.

Unfortunately, a California Coastal Trail leading from the Mexican border to the Oregon border would, by most estimates, need to be substantially longer than 800 miles— probably at least 1,600 miles long—and would visit a lot of places coast lovers would probably rather not see. Dreaming about a California Coastal Trail brings up a dilemma: Is the glass half-empty or half-full? That is, should we take pleasure in those parts of "the greatest meeting of land and sea in the world" preserved in parks, or should we stand aghast at the coastal carnage and embark on a course of political action to preserve what is threatened?

The answer, I think, is to enjoy and preserve California's coastline. In fact, for the coast walker, these activities are almost invariably intertwined.

The author, in many other forums in many other publications, has pointed his finger at oil drillers, forest destroyers, greedy developers and dumb bureaucrats. This publication, however, is a book about walking California's coast—the most beautiful and most inspiring parts of the state's shoreline and coastal mountains. Editorializing and finger-pointing in this volume has been kept to a minimum, primarily because it's the author's belief that the coast walker who truly cares, will rise, unprompted, to the defense of our shores.

To be sure, all is not splendid along the one hundred paths described in this book. In Orange County, you'll encounter a wetland that, after years of oil-drilling activity, is slowly being restored. From atop King's Peak, you'll overlook a lot of bald hills, shorn by destructive clear-cut logging operations.

I have deliberately steered the reader away from places such as Laguna Beach, where a Maginot Line of barbed wire and concrete thwarts the coast walker. I have avoided nuclear power plants, condo-contaminated coastline, and broccoli fields patrolled by cranky farmers. For the most part, this book takes good trails to lovely places.

Good trails, it must be emphasized, are a precious commodity. Besides a trail's obvious recreational and educational value, a trail can be seen as a kind of miner's canary. Miners of old kept an eye on their caged canary; if the bird died it meant that environmental conditions were poor. Trails, too, can be seen as an indicator of environmental conditions. When people are walking a beach, bluff, or mountain trail, there is likely a constituency that cares about the past, present and future of the land this trail crosses. Conversely, when a trail is closed or coastal access denied, you can bet that some land misuse or abuse will soon follow.

Trails are made, not born. Many paths were constructed more than a half-century ago during the Depression by the Civilian Conservation Corps, and have since received only sporadic maintenance. Regrettably, because of budget cutbacks and benign neglect, the state of the state's trail system can at best be described as mediocre.

As an investment in the future of the state, as a commitment to ensuring that the next generation has the opportunity to walk to the same places you now enjoy, volunteer a little time to help build or maintain a trail. State and federal park rangers, as well as independent trails advocacy groups often sponsor "Trail Days," which coordinate volunteers to work a stretch of trail. It's hard, but satisfying work, and you'll have a good time meeting fellow trails enthusiasts.

While out coast walking, if you happen across a neglected, hazardous or overgrown trail, or a trail being massacred by off-road vehicles or mountain bicycles, please report it to the relevant ranger or administrator. Only if you make your feelings known will conditions improve.

The coast's future depends not only on lawmakers and Coastal Commissioners, but to a large extent on citizens adopting a new visualization, another way of looking at land and sea, a vision of the coastline not as a sandbox for play, but as a living thing placed in our trust. Until a new visualization is generally accepted, the problems of zoning, population density, cliff collapse, sewage discharge, and oil drilling will be extremely difficult to solve. Until a new visualization is adopted, the forces of Cut & Fill and Grade & Pave will continue their assaults against landmark and landscape. Until we instill in our citizenry a sense of history, beauty and natural proportion, the present path of vulgarization and defilement of the California coast will continue.

One very good way to develop an ecologically sound vision for the coastline is to walk it—to see the shore in its many moods and manifestations. I hope that, in some modest way, this book contributes to a new vision.

Equipping for a Coast Walk

A long discussion of hiking equipment is beyond the scope of this guide. There are many good books on the subject. However, coast and coast range walking creates some special equipment needs:

Day Packs: A good one will last a lifetime. Bike bags or book bags of cotton or thin nylon won't hold up well. Shoulder pads and a hip band for support are nice features. Get one with a tough covered zipper. Double-O rings slip and aren't the greatest shoulder strap adjusters. Get tabler buckles; they don't slip, and they adjust quickly.

Footwear: Leave those three-pound mountaineering boots at home. Investigate the new running shoe-hiking boot hybrids. They offer more support and stability than a running shoe, yet are amazingly light and well ventilated. They vary in style; some look like reinforced running shoes, others like hiking boots with fabric uppers. Look for a good sturdy toe box.
   A disadvantage of the new lightweights—and the proliferation of new "walking shoes" on the market—is that they're not waterproof, a consideration if you're walking one of the coast range trails in winter. They are water repellent, however, and will get you through wet meadows and mudflats.

Clothing: A T-shirt and a cotton shirt that buttons down will give you a lot of temperature-regulating possibilities. Add a wool sweater, and a windbreaker with a hood, and you'll be protected against the sudden changes of temperature that often occur on the coast and in the coast ranges.

* Shorts are useful to the southern and central California coast walker much of the year.

* Hats offer protection from the sun, and protect against heat loss when the weather is cold.

* Sunglasses are particularly needed when one walks over white sands or on hot, explosed slopes. Even an overcast day can create a lot of glare.

* Rain gear—For the ultimate is protection and freedom of movement, a Gore-tex or similar type rainsuit is a good investment, particularly if you coast walk during the rainy season.

First Aid Kit: Take along a standard kit, supplemented with an ace bandage in the event of hiker's knee or sprained ankle. Take moleskin for blisters. Sunscreen or tanning lotion will keep you from getting burned, and is absolutely essential for the fair-skinned.

Water: It's still possible to drink from some coast range springs and streams without ill effect, but each individual water source should be carefully scrutinized. Many walkers assume water is pure, and 48 hours later have a queasy feeling that tells them their assumption was wrong. Water may harbor the organism Giardia Lamblia, one of the causes of "traveler's diarrhea." When you approach a water source, think about what may be upstream. A campground? Cows? Treat any backcountry water, if you have the slightest doubt about its quality.

Maps: The maps in this guide are sufficient for most purposes, particularly for walks that follow the beach. To get "the big picture," obtain the appropriate state park, national park, and national forest maps. You may also wish to pack a few topographic maps when hiking in the coast ranges.

Tide Tables: There are two high tides and two low tides every 24 hours 50 minutes. (It would be convenient for walkers to make it an even 24 hours, but the tides are governed by the gravitational pull of the moon and sun—over which we have no control.)

The times of these high and low tides are predicted and published each year by the U.S. Hydrographic Office. Newspapers usually publish the times of high and low tides. Local tide booklets are available free from many marine hardware stores, dive shops, and sporting goods stores. Having the right tide table in your possession is important, because some coast walks are difficult, even impassable, at high tide.

As you travel the coast, you must pick up a new tide booklet every hundred miles or so, for a tidebook issued for Mendocino has no more value in San Diego than a Utah road map. Last year's tide table is no more useful than last year's calendar.

The time to go coast walking, tidepool exploring, or seashell collecting, is at low tide. You'll want to plan your day so that you begin walking a few hours before low tide and finish a few hours after.

16

Precautions on the Trail

Poison Oak: This infamous plant grows abundantly through the coastal ranges up to an elevation of 5,000 feet and is present on many ocean bluff trails. It may lurk under other shrubs or take the form of a vine and climb up a redwood or an oak.

Poison oak's three-lobed leaves resemble leaves of the true oak. The leaves are one to four inches long and glossy, as if waxed.

All parts of the plant at all times of the year contain poisonous sap that can severely blister skin and mucous membranes. Its sap is most toxic during spring and summer. In fall, poison oak is particularly conspicuous, its leaves turning to flaming crimson or orange. However, its color change is more a response to heat and dryness than season; its "fall color" can occur anytime, particularly in Southern California. In winter, poison oak is naked, its stalks blending into the dull hue of the backcountry.

Contrary to popular belief, you can't catch poison oak from someone else's rash, but petting an animal, or handling a piece of clothing that carries it, can make you a victim.

There are a multitude of remedies. At the first opportunity, wash with soap and water. A bath with one-half cup sea salt and one-half cup of kelp helps dry the oozing. A dip in the ocean can help too. A few tablespoons of baking soda added to a tub of lukewarm water calms the itchies as well. Mugwort is also an effective treatment. Its fresh juice applied directly to the pained area relieves itching. Then, of course, there are always calamine lotion, and cortisone cream.

Rattlesnakes: Despite the common fear of rattlers, few people see them and rarely is anyone bitten. The red diamond and Southern Pacific rattlesnakes are found in coastal regions.

Getting to a hospital emergency room is more important than any other first aid. Keep the site of the wound as immobilized as possible, and relax. Cutting and suction treatments are now medically out of vogue, and advised only as a last resort if you're absolutely sure you can't get to a hospital within four hours.

Ticks: They're one-quarter inch long, and about the same color as the ground, so they're hard to see. Ticks are usually picked up by brushing against low vegetation. When hiking in a tick area, it's best to sit on rocks rather than fallen logs. Check your skin and clothing occasionally. If one is attached to the skin, it should be lifted off with a gentle pull. Before bathing, look for ticks on the body, particularly in the hair and pubic region.

Precautions in the Surf

Stingrays may be encountered, particularly in late summer. They lie about the bottom in the surf zone, and if stepped on, may inflict a painful wound. If stung, cleanse the area thoroughly to avoid infection.

Sea urchins appear in rocky tidal zones. Armored with brittle purple spines, they grow 2 to 6 inches in diameter. If you step on an urchin, the spines break off. You must remove the mildly poisonous spines with great care, because if allowed to remain under the skin, they'll make the wound hurt for a long time. Dissolve the spines, which are made of calcium carbonate, in a weak acid such as vinegar, lemon juice, or, uh...uric acid. The latter suggests possible first aid procedure on an isolated beach.

Jellyfish are common in the summer months. Avoid them. Their clear blue or purple umbrella-shaped floats are less than a foot in diameter, but their stinging tentacles may dangle ten or fifteen feet below the surface. Traditional first aid is to rub the affected area with wet sand, wash it with ammonia, and apply burn ointment.

18

Conservation of Marine Life

Some general rules should be remembered whenever one is observing marine organisms. Rocks, which have been turned over, should be replaced in their original position, otherwise the plants and animals which were originally on the upper surface are now on the bottom and will die; the same, in reverse, holds for animals that were originally on the bottom of the rock.

Whenever digging in the sand or mud for clams or other creatures, the material should be shoveled back into the hole because many organisms die when their habitat is disturbed. Remember, each species has its own specific habitat, and whenever we disturb its environment, chances are the organism will die.

Michael Jacobs/MJP

Kids and Hollywood Stars unite to save Santa Monica Bay during the Children's March sponsored by Heal the Bay.

SOUTH COAST

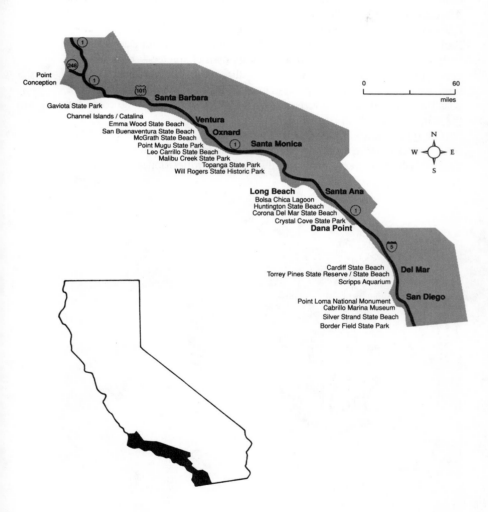

Point
Conception

Gaviota State Park

Channel Islands / Catalina
Emma Wood State Beach
San Buenaventura State Beach
McGrath State Beach
Point Mugu State Park
Leo Carrillo State Beach
Malibu Creek State Park
Topanga State Park
Will Rogers State Historic Park

Santa Barbara

Ventura

Oxnard

Santa Monica

Long Beach
Bolsa Chica Lagoon
Huntington State Beach
Corona Del Mar State Beach
Crystal Cove State Park
Dana Point

Santa Ana

Cardiff State Beach
Torrey Pines State Reserve / State Beach
Scripps Aquarium

Del Mar

Point Loma National Monument
Cabrillo Marina Museum
Silver Strand State Beach
Border Field State Park

San Diego

0   60
miles

N
W   E
S

21

SOUTH COAST

Since before the turn-of-the-century, when inland farmers took their families to the beach to camp out and cool off, the San Diego, Orange, Los Angeles, Ventura, and Santa Barbara shores have served as resort areas for California residents. Many of the "watering places" of old are still popular— Balboa Island, La Jolla, Laguna, Venice, Ventura and Santa Barbara.

Each Southern California beach has its own character— best surfing, clearest water, panoramic view, most birdlife. The air and water temperatures are Mediterranean, the place-names Spanish. It's easy to see why the coastline is an attraction for visitors from around the world, who come for the sun, sand, and historical romance.

The typical mass-use Southern California beach includes acres of hot sand, waves ranging from the gentle to the inspired, a lifeguard stationed every few hundred feet, and a boardwalk full of roller skaters, restaurants

and raft rental establishments. Before dawn, huge mechanized sand rakes scoop up trash, doing a good job of picking up after sloppy beach-goers.

Millions flock to the promised sand, and most cluster blanket-to-blanket on the same few beaches. The less-accessible beaches, bluffs, and coastal ridges are left to those willing to walk.

For the coast walker, the south coast offers not only those white sand beaches depicted on postcards, but a wide variety of shoreline features—the palms of La Jolla and Santa Monica, the cliffs of Torrey Pines State Reserve and Palos Verdes Peninsula. Above Santa Barbara, the Santa Ynez Mountains march toward the Pacific and at Point Mugu, the Santa Monica Mountains do likewise.

Northern San Diego is one of the south coast's special places to walk. A shoreline of sandy beaches and sandstone bluffs is broken up by scattered lagoons. Many of Southern California's valuable wetlands are here: Penasquito, Buena Vista, Batequitos. On the bluffs south of Del Mar, grow the rare Torrey pines, set aside in a reserve that shelters a remnant of the south coast of two hundred years ago: Paradise before the fall.

Southern California is blessed with several islands. Located 22 miles offshore, Catalina, with its steep brush and cactus-covered ridges, clear waters and beautiful coves, is a walker's delight. Most of the island, except for the resort town of Avalon, is rural, the domain of buffalo, boar and backpackers.

Ventura Harbor is the home of Channel Islands National Park. Visitors sail to San Miguel, Santa Rosa, Santa Cruz, Santa Barbara and Anacapa Islands to view the sea elephants, enjoy the giant coreopsis in bloom, and watch the migrating whales.

Another highlight for the coast walker, is the Santa Monica Mountains, the only relatively undeveloped mountain range that bisects a major metropolitan area. The mountains stretch from Griffith Park in the heart of the Los Angeles to Point Mugu, fifty miles away. State and national parklands host a rich pastiche of nature paths, scenic overlooks, fire roads, and horse trails leading through diverse ecosystems: native tall grass prairie, fern-lined canyons, rugged, rocky ridgetops.

The south coast walker will find one sandy and mellow beach after another. But expect some surprises. Though a huge metropolis crowds the shoreline, there are still some amazingly tranquil and pretty places awaiting your discovery.

23

▲ 1
Border Field Trail

Border Field State Park to Tijuana River: 3 miles round trip
Border Field State Park to Imperial Beach: 6 miles round trip

Border Field Trail begins at the very southwest corner of America, at the monument marking the border between Mexico and California. When California became a territory at the end of the Mexican-American War, an international border became a necessity. American and Mexican survey crews determined the boundary, and the monument of Italian marble was placed in 1851 to mark the original survey site. Today the monument stands in the shadow of the Tijuana Bull Ring and still delineates the border between the United States and Estados Unidos Mexicanos.

During World War II, the Navy used Border Field as an airfield. Combat pilots received gunnery training, learning to hit steam-driven targets that raced over the dunes on rails called Rabbit Tracks. Despite multifarious real estate schemers, the Navy retained control of Border Field until the land was given to the state in the early 1970s.

Before you walk down the bluffs to the beach, take in the panoramic view: the Otay Mountains and the San Miguel Mountains to the east, Mexico's Coronado Islands out to sea, and to the north—the Tijuana River flood plain, the Silver Strand, Coronado.

Much of the Tijuana River Estuary, one of the few salt marshes left in Southern California and one of the region's most important bird habitats, is within Border Field's boundaries.

This walk explores the dune and estuary ecosystems of the state park and takes you to wide sandy Imperial Beach. Wear an old pair of shoes and be prepared for the soft mud of the marsh.

Directions to the trailhead: Border Field State Park is located in the southwestern corner of California, with Mexico and the Pacific Ocean as its southern and western boundaries. From Interstate 5 (San Diego Freeway) south, exit on Hollister Street, proceed to a T-intersection, bear west (right) 2 miles on Monument Road to the state park. The park closes at sunset.

The Walk: Follow the short bluff trail down to the beach, which is under strict 24-hour surveillance by the U.S. Border Patrol. The beach is usually deserted, quite a contrast to crowded Tijuana Beach a few hundred yards to the south. As you walk north on Border Field State Park's 1 1/2-mile-long beach, you'll pass sand dunes anchored by salt grass, pickleweed and sand

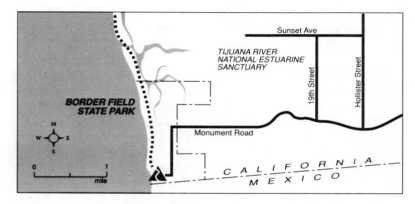

verbena. On the other side of the dunes is the Tijuana River Estuary, an essential breeding ground, feeding and nesting spot for more than 170 species of native and migratory birds. At Border Field, the salt marsh is relatively unspoiled, unlike so many wetlands encountered farther north, which have been drained, filled or used as dumps.

Take time to explore the marsh. You may spot marsh hawk, brown pelican, California gull, black-necked stilt, snowy egret, western sandpiper and American kestrel—to name a few of the more common birds. Fishing is good for perch, corbina and halibut both in the surf along Border Field Beach and in the estuary.

A mile and a half from the border you'll reach the mouth of the Tijuana River. Only after heavy storms is the Tijuana River the wide swath pictured on some maps. Most of the time it's fordable at low tide, but use your best judgement.

Continue north along wide, sandy Imperial Beach, past some houses and low bluffs. Imperial Beach was named by the South San Diego Investment Company to lure Imperial Valley residents to build summer cottages on the beach. Waterfront lots could be purchased for $25 down, $25 monthly and developers promised the balmy climate would "cure rheumatic proclivities, catarrhal trouble, lesions of the lungs," and an assortment of other ailments.

In more recent times, what was once a narrow beach protected by a seawall has been widened considerably by sand dredged from San Diego Bay. There's good swimming and surfing along Imperial Beach, where the waves can get huge. The beach route reaches Imperial Pier, built in 1912 and the oldest in the county.

2

Bayside Trail

Old Point Loma Lighthouse to Cabrillo National Monument Boundary:
2 miles round trip

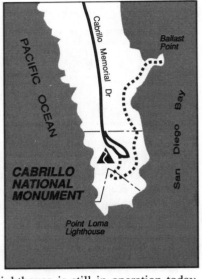

Cabrillo National Monument, on the tip of Point Loma, marks the point where Portuguese navigator Juan Rodriguez Cabrillo became the first European to set foot on California soil. He landed near Ballast Point in 1542 and claimed San Diego Bay for Spain. Cabrillo liked this "closed and very good port" and said so in his report to the King of Spain.

One highlight of a visit to the national monument is the Old Point Loma Lighthouse. This lighthouse, built by the federal government, first shined its beacon in 1855. Because fog often obscured the light, the station was abandoned in 1891 and a new one was built on lower ground at the tip of Point Loma. The 1891 lighthouse is still in operation today, operated by the Coast Guard. The 1855 lighthouse has been wonderfully restored to the way it looked when Captain Israel and his family lived there in the 1880s.

Bayside Trail begins at the old lighthouse and winds past yucca and prickly pear, sage and buckwheat. The Monument protects one the last patches of native flora in southernmost California, a hint at how San Diego Bay may have looked when Cabrillo's two small ships anchored here.

Directions to trailhead: Exit Interstate 5 on Rosecrans Street (Highway 209 south) and follow the signs to Cabrillo National Monument. There is a small entry fee.

Cabrillo National Monument opens daily at 9:00 a.m.

Old Point Loma Lighthouse

The Walk: Before embarking on this easy family hike, you may want to obtain a trail guide at the visitors center. The guide describes the coastal sage and chaparral communities, as well as local history.

The first part of the Bayside Trail winding down from the old lighthouse is a paved road. At a barrier, you bear left on a gravel road, once a military patrol road. During World War II, the Navy secreted bunkers and searchlights along these coastal bluffs.

Bayside Trail provides fine views of the San Diego Harbor shipping lanes. Sometimes when Navy ships pass, park rangers broadcast descriptions of the vessels. Also along the trail is one of Southern California's most popular panoramic views: miles of seashore, 6,000-foot mountains to the east and Mexico to the south.

The trail dead-ends at the park boundary.

Return the same way.

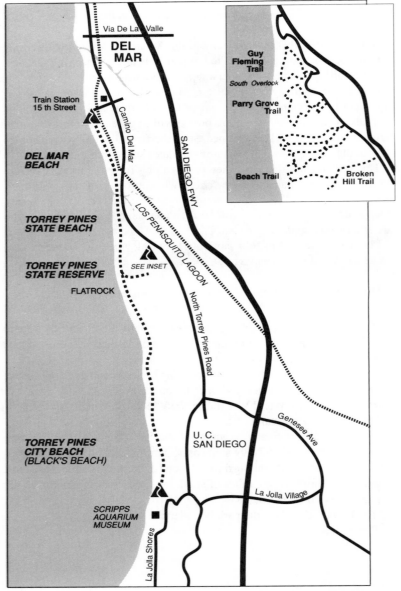

Trails 3, 4, & 5

3

Torrey Pines Beach Trail

Scripps Pier to Torrey Pines State Beach: 10 miles round trip

Before or after this walk, check out the Aquarium Museum at Scripps Institute of Oceanography. In the Aquarium, all manner of local sea creatures are on display. Underwater video cameras provide views of activity in the nearby marine reserve. Located near the entrance of the Aquarium is a dryland tidepool, where the tide rises and falls in 2-hour intervals. Kelp planted in the pools provides hiding places for bright orange garibaldi, rock-fish, and red snapper. Starfish, barnacles, and sea anenomes cling to the rocks. A wave generator simulates surf conditions.

This walk begins at Scripps Pier, passes along Torrey Pines City Beach, known locally as Black's Beach, once swimsuit-optional, now enforced suits-only. After walking below some spectacular cliffs and along Torrey Pines State Beach, you'll arrive at Torrey Pines State Reserve, home to the rare and revered *pinus Torreyana.*

Plan your hike for low tide, particularly during winter when beach sand is carried away by high waves.

Directions to trailhead: Exit Interstate 5 on La Jolla Village Drive, traveling west past UC San Diego to North Torrey Pines Rd. Turn right, then make a left on La Jolla Shores Drive, follow it to the Aquarium turnoff on your right. Parking is sparse and metered near the Aquarium.

The Walk: As you look south from Scripps Pier, you'll see long and flat La Jolla Shores Beach, a wide expanse of white sand where the water deepens gradually. This is a family beach, popular during the summer with swimmers.

Walking north, the going is rocky at first; the surf really kicks up around Scripps Pier. Soon the beach widens, growing more sandy, and the spectacular curry-colored cliffs grow higher and higher.

A glider port once stood atop the bluffs. Manned fixed-wing gliders were pulled into the air, and they rode the currents created by onshore breezes rising up as they meet the cliffs. Nowadays, brave adventurers strap themselves to hang gliders and leap off the cliffs and, unless the wind shifts, come to a soft landing on the beach below.

The 300-foot cliffs tower over Black's Beach, named for William Black, Sr., the oil millionaire who owned and developed most of the land on the cliffs. During the 1970s, Black's Beach enjoyed fleeting notoriety as the first

and only public beach in the country on which nudity was legal. Called "a noble experiment" by sun worshipers and "a terrible fiasco" by the more inhibited, the clothing-optional zone was defeated at the polls.

After passing below more handsome bluffs, you'll spot a distinct rock outcropping called Flat Rock. Here you may join a bluff trail that leads up to Torrey Pines State Reserve.

4

Torrey Pines State Reserve Trails

Atop the bluffs of Torrey Pines State Reserve lies a microcosm of old California, a garden of shrubs and succulents.

Most visitors come to view the 3,000 or so *pinus Torreyana*, but the Reserve also offers the walker a striking variety of native plants, If you enjoy interpretive nature trails, the Reserve has some nice ones. Protect the fragile ecology of the area by staying on established paths.

Be sure to check out the interpretive displays at the park museum and the native plant garden near the head of the Parry Grove Trail. Plant and bird lists, as well as wildflower maps (Feb.-June) are available for a small fee.

Among the reserve trails: (See page 28 for map)

Parry Grove Trail, named in honor of Dr. C. C. Parry, takes you through a handsome grove of Torrey pines. Parry was a botanist assigned to the boundary commission that surveyed the Mexican-American border in 1850. While waiting for the expedition to start, Parry explored the San Diego area. He investigated a tree that had been called the Soledad pine for the nearby Soledad Valley. Parry sent samples to his teacher and friend, Dr. John Torrey of Princeton, and asked that if it proved to be a new species, it be named for Torrey. The Soleded pine became *pinus Torreyana*, or Torrey pine, in honor of the famous botanist and taxonomist.

The 4/10-mile loop trail also leads past many kinds of plants in the reserve: toyon, yucca, and other coastal shrubs.

Broken Hill Trail visits a drier chaparral-dominated landscape, full of sage and buckwheat, ceanothus and manzanita. From Broken Hill overlook, there's a view of a few Torrey pines clinging to life in an environment that resembles a desert badlands.

Beach Trail leads to Yucca Point and Razor Point and offers precipitous views of the beach below. The trail descends the bluffs to Flat Rock, a fine tidepool area.

Guy Fleming Trail is 6/10-mile loop that travels through stands of Torrey pine and takes you to South Overlook, where you might glimpse a migrating California gray whale.

31

Del Mar Beach Trail

Train Station to Torrey Pines State Reserve: 6 miles round trip

Along Del Mar Beach, the power of the surf is awesome and cliff collapse unpredictable. At this beach, permeable layers of rock tilt toward the sea and lie atop other impermeable layers. Water percolates down through the permeable rock, settles on the impermeable rock and "greases the skids"— and ideal condition for collapsing cliffs.

On New Year's Day in 1941, a freight train suddenly found itself in midair. Erosion had undermined the tracks. A full passenger train had been delayed, so the freight train's crew of three were the only casualties.

This walk takes you along the beach, visits the superb Flat Rock tidepool, and detours up the bluffs to Torrey Pines State Reserve. At the Reserve, you'll see those relics from the Ice Age, Torrey Pines, which grow only atop the Del Mar bluffs and on Santa Barbara Island; no other place in the world.

Consult a tide table and schedule your walk at low tide when there's more beach to walk and tidepool life is easier to observe.

Directions to trailhead: (See page 28 for map) By train: Board a southbound train at Los Angeles' Union Station or another station along the line, and get off in Del Mar. Reservations are usually not necessary. Amtrak fares and schedules: (800) 872-7245.

By car: From Interstate 5 in Del Mar, exit on Via de la Valle. Continue west to Highway S21 and turn left (south) along the ocean past the race tracks and fairgrounds to reach the train station. If you can't find a place to park at the train station, park in town.

The Walk: From the train station, cross the tracks to the beach and begin hiking south. With the high cliffs on your left and the pounding breakers on your right, you'll feel you're entering another world. Follow the sometimes wide, sometimes narrow beach over sparkling sand and soft green limestone rock. Holes in the limestone are evidence of marine life that once made its home there.

You'll hike past a couple of numbered lifeguard towers. When you reach Tower 5, turn left and make a brief detour through the Highway S21 underpass to Los Penasquitos Lagoon, a saltwater marsh patrolled by native and migratory waterfowl. After observing the least terns and light-footed clapper rails, return to the beach trail.

After three miles of beachcombing, you'll see a distinct rock outcropping, named appropriately enough, Flat Rock. Legend has it that this gouged-out rock, also known as Bathtub Rock, was the site of a luckless Scottish miner's search for coal. Common tidepool residents housed in the rocks at the base of the bluff include barnacles, mussels, crabs and sea anemones.

Just north of Flat Rock, a stairwell ascends the bluffs to Torrey Pines State Reserve. Torrey pines occupy the bold headlands atop the yellow sandstone; these rare and graceful trees seem to thrive on the foggy atmosphere and precarious footing. The Reserve features superb nature trails, native plant gardens and interpretive exhibits.

pinus Torreyana

6

Moro Canyon Trail

Park Headquarters to top of Moro Canyon: 7 miles round trip; 700-foot elevation gain

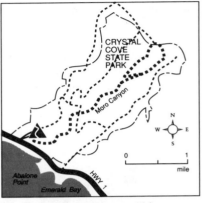

Extending three miles along the coast between Laguna Beach and Corona del Mar, and inland over the San Joaquin Hills, 3,000-acre Crystal Cove State Park attracts birdwatchers, beachcombers and hikers.

The backcountry of Crystal Cove State Park is part of the San Joaquin Hills, first used by Mission San Juan Capistrano for grazing land. Cattle raising continued under Jose Sepulveda when the area became part of his land grant, Rancho San Joaquin, in 1837. In 1864, Sepulveda sold the land to James Irvine and his partners and it became part of his Irvine Ranch. Grazing continued until shortly after the state purchased the property as parkland in 1979.

Former Irvine Ranch roads now form a network of hiking trails that loop through the state park. An especially nice trail travels the length of Moro Canyon, the main watershed of the park. An oak woodland, a seasonal stream and sandstone caves are some of the attractions of a walk through this canyon. Birdwatchers may spot the roadrunner, quail, Cooper's hawk, California thrasher, wrentit and many more species.

After exploring inland portions of the state park, allow some time to visit the park's coastline, highlighted by grassy bluffs, sandy beaches, tidepools and coves. The Pelican Point, Crystal Cove, Reef Point and Moro Beach areas of the park allow easy beach access. An offshore area adjacent to the park has been designated an underwater park for divers.

Directions to trailhead: Crystal Cove State Park is located off Highway 1, about two miles south of the town of Corona del Mar or one mile north of Laguna Beach. Turn inland on the short park road, signed "El Moro Canyon." Drinking water, restrooms, interpretive displays and plenty of parking are available at the ranger station.

Park hours are 6:30 a.m. to sunset. There is an entrance fee. Pick up a trails map at the ranger station. At the station, you can consult the schedule of ranger-led interpretive walks, which explore both inland and coastal sections of the state park. More park information: (714) 494-3539.

The Walk: Below the ranger station, near the park entry kiosk, pick up the unsigned Moro Canyon Trail, which crosses the grassy slopes behind a school and trailer park down into Moro Canyon. At the canyon bottom, you meet a fire road and head left, up-canyon.

The walker may observe such native plants as black sage, prickly pear cactus, monkey flowers, golden bush, lemonade berry and deer weed. Long before Spanish missionaries and settlers arrived in Southern California, a native Indian population flourished in the coastal canyons of Orange County. The abundance of edible plants in the area, combined with the mild climate and easy access to the bounty of the sea, contributed to the success of these people, whom archaeologists believe lived off this land for more than four thousand years.

The canyon narrows and you ignore fire roads joining Moro Canyon from the right and left. You stay in the canyon bottom and proceed through an oak woodland, which shades a trickling stream. You'll pass a shallow sandstone cave just off the trail to the right.

About 2 1/2 miles from the trailhead, you'll reach the unsigned junction with a fire road. If you wish to make a loop trip out of this day hike, bear left on this road, which climbs steeply west, then northeast toward the ridgetop that forms a kind of inland wall for Muddy, Moro, Emerald and other coastal canyons.

When you reach the ridgetop, unpack your lunch and enjoy the far reaching views of the San Joaquin Hills and Orange County coast, Catalina and San Clemente Islands. You'll also have a raven's eye view of Moro Canyon and the route back to the trailhead. After catching your breath, you'll bear right (east) along the ridgetop and quickly descend back into Moro Canyon. A 3/4-mile walk brings you back to the junction where you earlier ascended out of the canyon. This time you continue straight down-canyon, retracing your steps to the trailhead.

7

Crystal Cove Trail

Reef Point to Crystal Cove: 2 miles round trip
Reef Point to Pelican Point: 4 miles round trip

Trails 7 & 8

Orange County's—in fact, the Southland's—largest stretch of undeveloped coastline lies within the boundaries of Crystal Cove State Park. The park's 3 1/4-mile long sandy beach, bisected by rocky points, is backed by dramatic sandstone bluffs. Both beach and bluffs offer fine walking routes.

After Pacific Coast Highway was completed in the 1920s, Japanese-American truck farmers worked the coastal slopes. They grew vegetables and sold them from roadside produce stands along the highway.

The James Irvine Ranch, which has owned most of the land in the area since the days of the great ranchos, made extensive use of the San Joaquin Hills for its cattle raising operation. The cows grazing on nearby slopes create a pastoral scene and are an ever-increasing anomaly on the urban Orange County coast. The coastal slopes face heavy development pressure and an uncertain future.

Directions to trailhead: Crystal Cove State Park is located between the towns of Corona Del Mar and Laguna Beach. Turn west off Pacific Coast Highway into the Reef Point day use area. There is a parking fee.

The Walk: From the parking area, head north along the bluffs, which are dotted with coreopsis and black sage. The state park is attempting to restore the native vegetation, which was altered by livestock and the introduction of non-native grasses.

Descend the coastal accessway to the beach and continue your walk along the sandy shore. A short distance north is a fine tidepool area. The intertidal zone and near shore waters here have been designated the Irvine Coast Marine Life Refuge.

Beyond the tidepools is the tiny resort community of Crystal Cove, site of a few dozen beach cottages. The wood frame cottages have been little altered since their construction in the 1920s and were recently collectively named to the National Register of Historic Places. "Cove" is something of a misnomer because the beach here shows almost no coastal indentation.

You may continue beach walking another mile to Pelican Point, where a coastal accessway allows you to return to the bluff tops. You may walk south atop the bluffs back to Crystal Cove, where you can then return to the beach.

As you return to Reef Point, you'll get a good view south of Abalone Point. This rocky promontory, located just outside Laguna Beach city limits is made of eroded lava and other volcanic material distributed in the San Joaquin Hills. It's capped by a grass-covered dome rising two hundred feet above the water. North of the point is El Moro Beach, a part of Crystal Cove State Park. The sandy beach is sometimes beautifully cusped. El Moro is a misspelling of the Spanish word morro, meaning round, and describes the round dome of Abalone Point.

Ascend the second, southernmost Reef Point coastal accessway and return to the day use area where you began.

8

Crown of the Sea Trail

Corona Del Mar Beach to Arch Rock: 2 miles round trip
Corona Del Mar Beach to Crystal Cove: 4 miles round trip
Corona Del Mar Beach to Abalone Point: 7 miles round trip

In 1904, George Hart purchased 700 acres of land on the cliffs east of the entrance to Newport Bay and laid out a subdivision he called Corona Del Mar ("Crown of the Sea"). The only way to reach the townsite was by way of a long muddy road that circled around the head of Upper Newport Bay. Later a ferry carried tourists and residents from Balboa to Corona Del Mar. Little civic improvement occurred until Highway 101 bridged the bay and the community was annexed to Newport Beach.

This walk explores the beaches and marine refuges of "Big" and Little Corona Del Mar Beaches and continues to the beaches of Crystal Cove State Park.

Directions to trailhead: From Pacific Coast Highway in Corona Del Mar, turn oceanward on Marguerite Avenue, traveling a few blocks to Corona Del Mar State Beach. There is a fee for parking in the lot.

The Walk: Begin at the east jetty of Newport Beach, where you'll see sailboats tacking in and out of the harbor. Snorkelers and surfers frequent the rocky area of the jetty. Proceed down-coast along wide sandy Corona Del Mar State Beach.

The beach narrows as you approach the cove that encloses Little Corona Del Mar Beach. Snorkeling is good beneath the cliffs of "Big" and Little Corona beaches. Both areas are protected from boat traffic by kelp beds and marine refuge status.

A mile from the jetty, you'll pass well-named Arch Rock, which is just offshore and can be reached at low tide. The beach from Arch Rock to Irvine Cove, 2 1/2 miles to the south was purchased by the state from the Irvine Corporation and is now part of Crystal Cove State Park. Trails lead up the bluffs.

A mile's walk down the undeveloped beach brings you to Crystal Cove, a cluster of cottages between Pacific Coast Highway and the ocean at the mouth of Los Trancos Canyon.

Arch Rock

9

Back Bay Trail

3 1/2 miles one way

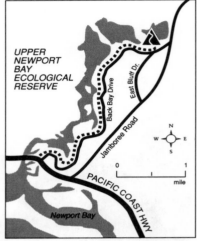

UPPER
NEWPORT
BAY
ECOLOGICAL
RESERVE

Back Bay Drive

East Bluff Dr.

Jamboree Road

Newport Bay

PACIFIC COAST HWY

0   1
mile

In 1974, Orange County and the Irvine Corporation reached an agreement calling for public ownership of Upper Newport Bay, most of which has become a state-operated ecological reserve. The Upper Bay is a marked contrast to the huge marina complex, one of the world's largest yacht harbors, of the Lower Bay—developments once planned for the Upper Bay. The preservation of Upper Newport Bay is one of Southern California conservationists' success stories.

The wetland is a premier bird-watching spot. Plovers stand motionless on one leg, great blue herons pick their way across the mudflats, flotillas of ducks patrol the shallows. Out of sight, mollusks, insects, fish and protozoa provide vital links in the complex food chain of the estuary.

This walk follows one-way Back Bay Drive which really should be closed to motorized traffic. However, on weekdays, there's rarely much traffic, and on weekends, there's seldom more auto traffic than bike traffic. The tideland is fragile; stay on established roads and trails.

Directions to trailhead: Turn inland off Pacific Coast Highway onto Jamboree Road, then left on Back Bay Drive. The road follows the margin of the bay. Park along the road.

The Walk: As you walk along the road, notice the various vegetation zones. Eel grass thrives in areas of almost constant submergence, cordgrasses at a few feet above mean low tide, salt wort and pickleweed higher on the banks of the estuary. Keep an eye out for three of California's endangered birds: Beldings Savanna Sparrow, the California least tern, the light-footed clapper rail. Old levees and an occasional trail let you walk out toward the main bodies of water. Also, a trail from the University of California at Irvine runs along the west side of the reserve.

41

10

Bolsa Chica Lagoon Trail

3 miles round trip

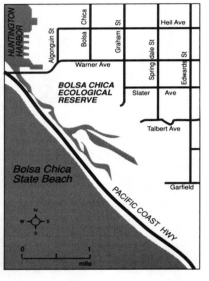

Bolsa Chica Wetlands, an 1,800-acre tidal basin surrounded by the city of Huntington Beach, is one of Southern California's most valuable oceanfront properties. The somewhat degraded marshland has been the scene of a long dispute between Signal Oil Company, the principal landholder, which would like to develop a marina and suburb, and Amigos de Bolsa Chica, who would like to preserve the marsh as a stopover for migratory birds on the Pacific Flyway and as a habitat for endangered species.

For many centuries, the wetlands were the bountiful home of Indians until a Mission-era land grant gave retiring Spanish soldier Manuel Nieto title to a portion of Bolsa Chica. Although the coastal marsh proved useless for farming and ranching to Nieto and succeeding owners, the abundant wildlife attracted game hunters from all over Southern California. At the turn of the century, the Bolsa Chica Gun Club, a group of Pasadena businessmen, acquired title to the land and created a hunting preserve. In order to stabilize their duck pond, they dammed off the ocean waters, thus starting the demise of the wetland.

In the 1920s, oil was discovered at Bolsa Chica. Dikes were built, water drained, wells drilled, roads spread across the marsh. In fact, oil production is scheduled to continue through the year 2020.

Portions of the marsh bordering Pacific Coast Highway have been restored by the state and are now part of an ecological preserve under Department of Fish and Game management. This loop trail takes you on a tour of the most attractive section. Bring your binoculars. Birding is quite good here.

Directions to trailhead: Bolsa Chica Ecological Reserve is located just opposite the main entrance of Bolsa Chica State Beach on Pacific Coast Highway. From the San Diego Freeway (405) exit on Beach Boulevard and follow it to the beach. Head north on Pacific Coast Highway for three miles to the Reserve entrance.

The Walk: At the trailhead is a sign giving some Bolsa Chica history. Cross the lagoon on the bridge, where other signs offer information about marshland plants and birds. The loop trail soon begins following a levee around the marsh. You'll pass fields of pickleweed and cordgrass, sun-baked mudflats, the remains of oil drilling equipment. Three endangered birds: Savanna sparrow, clapper rail, California least tern, are sometimes seen here.

At the north end of the loop, you may bear right on a closed road to an overlook. As you return, you cross the lagoon on another bridge and return to the parking area on a path paralleling Pacific Coast Highway.

Bird-watching, Bolsa Chica Lagoon

▲ 11
Bear Canyon Trail

Ortega Hwy to Pigeon Springs: 5 1/2 miles round trip; 700-foot gain
Ortega Hwy to Sitton Peak: 10 1/2 miles round trip; 1,300-foot gain

The Santa Ana Mountains may be the most overlooked and underutilized recreation area in Southern California. Stretching the entire length of Orange County's eastern perimeter, the Santa Anas roughly parallel the coast. A good part of the mountains lies within the boundaries of the Cleveland National Forest.

This coastal range is only about twenty miles inland, and the western slopes are often blanketed with fog. By midmorning, the sun scatters the fog into long colorful banners that invite you to some far-off parade. The coast has a cooling influence on what is often a very hot range of mountains.

Bear Canyon Trail offers a pleasant introduction to the Santa Ana Mountains. The trail climbs through gentle brush and meadow country, visits Pigeon Springs, and arrives at Four Corners, the intersection of several major hiking trails through the southern Santa Anas. One of these trails takes you to Sitton Peak for a fine view. Along the trail, refreshing Pigeon Springs welcomes hot and dusty hikers to a handsome oak glen.

Directions to trailhead: Take the Ortega Highway (California 74) turnoff from the San Diego Freeway (Interstate 5) at San Juan Capistrano. Drive east 20 miles to the paved parking area across from the Ortega Oaks store. Bear Canyon Trail starts just west of the store on Ortega Highway.

Departing from the parking lot is the 2-mile San Juan Loop Trail, another nice introduction to the Santa Ana Mountains.

You can obtain trail information and purchase a Cleveland National Forest map at El Cariso Station, located a few miles up Highway 74.

The Walk: From the signed trailhead, the broad, well-graded trail climbs slowly up brushy hillsides. The trail crosses a seasonal creek, which runs through a tiny oak woodland.

A half-mile from the trailhead, you'll enter the San Mateo Canyon Wilderness, set aside by Congress in 1984. The 40,000-acre preserve protects San Mateo Canyon, the crown jewel of the Santa Ana Mountains, a relatively untouched land of 200-year-old oaks, potreros, and quiet pools.

After a mile, a deceptive fork appears on the left. Ignore it. The trail climbs on, skirts the periphery of a meadow and crests a chaparral-covered slope. Just before the trail joins the Verdugo Trail, there's a nice view down into San Juan Canyon. Turn right (south) on Verdugo Trail and proceed 3/4 mile to Pigeon Springs.

Pigeon Springs includes a storage tank and horse trough. Forest rangers recommend that you purify the water before drinking. The springs are located among oaks on the left of the trail. If the bugs aren't biting, this can be a nice place to picnic.

Option: To continue on to Sitton Peak, hike down the Verdugo Trail another half-mile and you'll arrive at Four Corners, a convergence of trails (fire roads). The Verdugo Trail pushes straight ahead to an intersection with the Blue Water Trail. To the left is Blue Water Fire Road leading down to Fisherman's Camp in San Mateo Canyon. To proceed to Sitton Peak, bear right on the Sitton Peak Trail.

Follow the trail as it begins to climb and contour around the peak. There are a few trees up on the ridge but little shade en route. In a mile you'll be at the high point of Sitton Peak Trail, a saddle perched over San Juan Canyon. The high point of the trail is approximately at Forest Service marker W-56. Follow the trail another mile until you reach the southeast face of the peak. Leave the trail here and wend your way up past the rocky outcroppings to Sitton Peak. On a clear day, there are superb views of the twin peaks of Old Saddleback (Mt. Modjeska and Mt. Santiago), Mt. San Gorgonio and Mt. San Jacinto, Catalina and the wide Pacific.

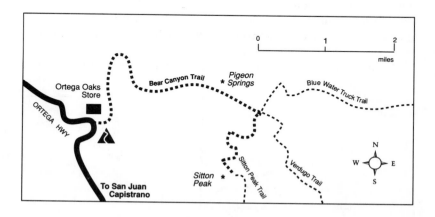

12

Cabrillo Beach Trail

Cabrillo Beach to White's Point: 3 miles round trip

All but forgotten, the rocky cove just down-coast from White's Point in San Pedro once flourished as a Roaring '20s health spa and resort. All that remain are some sea-battered cement ruins and lush overgrown gardens.

White's Point was originally settled at the turn of the century by immigrant Japanese fishermen who harvested the bountiful abalone from the waters off Palos Verdes Peninsula. Tons of abalone were shipped to the Far East and tons more were consumed locally in Los Angeles' Little Tokyo. In a few years the abalone was depleted, but an even greater resource was discovered at White's Point—sulfur springs.

In 1915, construction of a spa began. Eventually the large Royal Palms Hotel was built at water's edge. Palm gardens and a golf course decorated the cliffs above. The sulfur baths were especially popular with the Japanese population of Southern California.

The spa boomed in the '20s, but the 1933 earthquake closed the springs. The cove became part of Fort McArthur during World War II; the Japanese-American settlers were incarcerated in internment camps, and the resort was soon overwhelmed by crumbling cliffs and the powerful sea.

This walk begins at Cabrillo Beach, the only real sand beach for miles to the north and south, passes Cabrillo Marine Museum, and ends up at historic White's Point. For the most part, this walk stays atop the San Pedro and Palos Verdes Bluffs, but there's ample opportunity on this easy family excursion to descend to the sea. Your hiking and tidepool-viewing pleasure will be increased immeasurably if you walk during low tide.

Cabrillo Marine Museum is well worth a visit. It has marine displays,

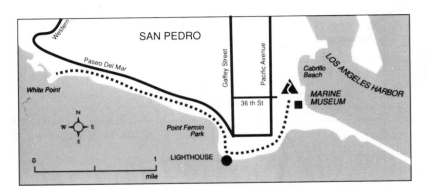

aquariums with live fish and good shell collections. One exhibit interprets the history of White's Point. The museum sponsors tidepool walks, grunion watches and is a coordinating point for whale watching cruises.

Directions to trailhead: Take the Harbor Freeway south to San Pedro and exit on Gaffey Street. Follow Gaffey seaward to 22nd and turn left. Turn right on Pacific Avenue and then left on 36th Street. Fee parking is available either near the museum or at Cabrillo Beach.

The Walk: Walk up sandy Cabrillo Beach, which has a monopoly on the grunion, since the sand-seeking fish have few other spawning options along Palos Verdes Peninsula. You'll soon pass the San Pedro breakwater and Cabrillo fishing pier. John Olguin, former Cabrillo Marine Museum Director, says that one of his favorite walks is atop the breakwater. "Great on a brisk winter day. Superb view of Los Angeles Harbor, and you might even spot a whale on the horizon."

Just up-coast from Cabrillo Beach is the rocky shoreline of Point Fermin Marine Life Refuge. Limpets, crabs and lobsters are a few of the many creatures found in the bountiful tidepools. After rock-hopping among the tidepools, you must follow a dirt path or the paved road up to the top of the coastal bluffs; it is all but impossible to walk around Point Fermin via the shoreline route. Walk uphill along Bluff Place to a parking lot at the terminus of Pacific Avenue and join a blufftop trail. This path takes you past remains of "Sunken City," a 1930s housing tract built on bluffs that soon collapsed. Palm trees and huge chunks of asphalt are all that remain of the ocean side housing tract.

Soon you'll arrive at Point Fermin Park and its handsome Victorian-style lighthouse, built in 1874 from materials shipped around Cape Horn. Shortly after the Japanese bombed Pearl Harbor, the lighthouse became an observation point.

Two coastal accessways lead down the park's bluffs to the rocky shoreline. As you near White's Point, you'll see a palm garden with fire pits. Royal Palms Hotel was once situated here until overcome by the sea. Storm-twisted palms and overgrown gardens are a reminder of flush times long passed. Royal Palms is a state beach popular with surfers.

Ahead at White's Point are some curious cement remains of the resort. Beyond the point stretch the rugged cliffs and cobblestone shores of Palos Verdes Peninsula. Return the same way or if you have the time, walk on. The difficult terrain will ensure that few follow in your footsteps.

47

13

Palos Verdes Peninsula Trail

Malaga Cove to Rocky Point: 5 miles round trip
Malaga Cove to Point Vincente Lighthouse: 10 miles round trip
Consult tidetable; hike at low tide

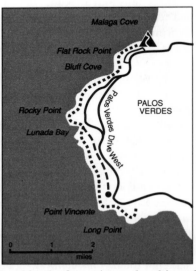

Geographically, the Palos Verdes bluffs and beaches resemble the Channel Islands. Geologists say that long ago, before the Ice Age began, the peninsula was an island, separated from the rest of Los Angeles basin by the sea. However, toward the end of the last glacial period, the eighteen-mile-long peninsula was connected to the mainland by masses of sediment discharged from the mountains to the north. The peninsula is famous for its rocky cliffs, which rise from 50 to 300 feet above the ocean and for its thirteen wave-cut terraces. These terraces, or platforms, resulted from a combination of uplift and sea-level fluctuations caused by the formation and melting of glaciers. Today the waves, as they have for so many thousands of years, are actively eroding the shoreline, cutting yet another terrace onto the land.

While enjoying this walk, you'll pass many beautiful coves, where whaling ships once anchored and delivered their cargo of whale oil. Large iron kettles, used to boil whale blubber, have been found in sea cliff caves, Indians, Spanish rancheros and Yankee smugglers have all added to the peninsula's romantic history. Modern times have brought white-stuccoed, red-tiled mansions to the peninsula bluffs, but the beach remains almost pristine. Offshore, divers explore the rocky bottoms for abalone and shellfish. Onshore, walkers enjoy the wave-scalloped bluffs and splendid tidepools.

Wear sturdy shoes on this walk. Hiking this beach is like walking over a surface of broken bowling balls. The route is rocky and progress slow, but that gives you more time to look down at the tidepools and up at the magnificent bluffs.

Point Vincente Lighthouse, built in 1926

Directions to trailhead: The narrow, rocky Palos Verdes beaches can be reached by a number of unofficial access points along Paseo Del Mar. To reach Malaga Cove trailhead, take Pacific Coast Highway to Palos Verdes Boulevard. Bear right on Palos Verdes Drive. As you near Malaga Cove Plaza, turn right at the first stop sign (Via Corta). Make a right on Via Arroyo, then another right into the parking lot behind the Malaga Cove School. The trailhead is on the ocean side of the parking area where a wide path descends the bluffs above the Flatrock Point tidepools. A footpath leaves from Paseo Del Mar, 1/10 mile past Via Horcada, where the street curves east to join Palos Verdes Drive West.

The Walk: From the Malaga Cove School parking lot, descend the wide path to the beach. A sign indicates you're entering a seashore reserve and asks you to treat tidepool residents with respect. To the north are sandy beaches for sedentary sun worshipers. Active rockhoppers clamber to the south. At several places along this walk you'll notice that the great terraces are cut by steep-walled canyons. The first of these canyon incisions can be observed at Malaga Cove, where Malaga Canyon slices through the north slopes of Palos Verdes Hills, then cuts west to empty at the cove.

The coastline curves out to sea in a southwesterly direction and Flatrock Point comes into view. The jade-colored waters swirl around this anvil-shaped point, creating the best tidepool area along this section of coast. Above the point, the cliffs soar to 300 feet. Cloaked in morning fog, the rocky seascape here is reminiscent of Big Sur.

Rounding Flatrock Point, you pick your way among the rocks, seaweed and the flotsam and jetsam of civilization to Bluff Cove, where sparkling combers explode against the rocks and douse the unwary with their tangy spray. A glance over your right shoulder brings a view of Santa Monica Bay, the Santa Monica Mountains in gray silhouette and on the far horizon, the Channel Islands.

A mile beyond Bluff Cove, Rocky (also called Palos Verdes) Point juts out like a ship's prow. Caught fast on the rocks at the base of the point is the rusting exoskeleton of the Greek freighter Dominator, a victim of the treacherous reef surrounding the peninsula.

Around Rocky Point is Lunada Bay, a good place to observe the terrace surfaces. From here you'll walk under almost perpendicular cliffs that follow horseshoe-shaped Lunada Bay. Shortly you'll round Resort Point, where fishermen try their luck. As the coastline turns south, Catalina can often be seen glowing on the horizon. Along this stretch of shoreline, numerous stacks, remnants of former cliffs not yet dissolved by the surf, can be seen.

The stretch of coast before the lighthouse has been vigorously scalloped by thousands of years of relentless surf. You'll have to boulderhop the last mile to Point Vincente. The lighthouse has worked its beacon over the dark waters since 1926.

Passage is sometimes impossible around the lighthouse at high tide. If the tide is passable, another 1/2-mile of walking brings you to an official beach access (or departure) route at Long Point.

14

Avalon Canyon Loop Trail

6 1/2 miles round trip: 1,000-foot elevation gain

The islophile expecting a lush landscape is often surprised by Catalina Island's backcountry. Catalina's vegetation is sparse, spartan. Catalina resembles a Greek island—one of the Cyclades, perhaps—far more than a tropical South Seas paradise.

Catalina shares the semi-arid conditions of Southern California, but hosts a surprising amount of plant life. About 600 species, 400 or so of them native plants, grow on the island. By taking a walk above Avalon, you can study the island's botany at the Botanical Garden, then venture into the interior to view Catalina's special flora in its natural habitat.

Each year about a million people travel to Catalina, but few of these visitors are hikers. The adventurer who strides out of Avalon will leave the crowds behind and be treated to superb island and mainland panoramic views.

The route out of Avalon, which I have dubbed, "Avalon Canyon Loop Trail," leads to the Botanical Garden, a showcase for plants native to Catalina and the Channel Islands. At the head of the canyon is the imposing Wrigley Memorial, a huge monument honoring chewing gum magnate William Wrigley, who purchased most of the island in 1919. Families with children and those visitors looking more for a walk than a hike will enjoy the trip as far as the Botanical Garden. More adventurous hikers will undertake

Avalon Harbor, turn-of-the-century view

51

the second, much more strenuous, part of this loop trip, which utilizes fire roads and Hermit Gulch Trail, and offers a sampling of Catalina's rugged and bold terrain.

Directions to trailhead: Several boat companies offer ferry service to and San Pedro. For more information about ferryboat schedules and island services/accomodations, call the Catalina Island Chamber of Commerce; (213) 510-1520.

If you intend to hike into the Catalina backcountry (anywhere past the Botanical Garden) you must secure a (free) hiking permit from the Los Angeles County Department of Parks and Recreation. The parks department operates an information center in the Island Plaza, located at 213 Catalina Street. You can pick up a trails map here and secure your permit. For more information about hiking the Catalina backcountry, call: (213) 510-0688

The Walk: Head uphill along Catalina Street, which soon joins Avalon Canyon Road, passes a few residences, and begins a 1 1/2 mile ascent toward the Botanical Garden. On your right, you'll soon pass one of William Wrigley's many contributions to the island, Bird Park, which once held thousands of unusual birds in the "largest bird cage in the world." Bird Park

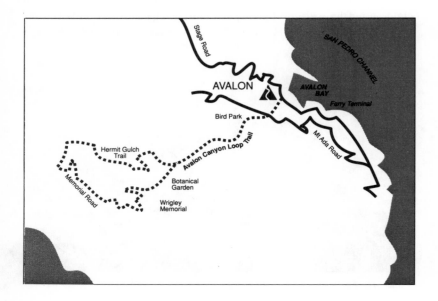

is now a campground. On the left side of the road, bleacher bums will stop and pay homage to the former spring training camp of Wrigley's beloved Chicago Cubs.

At the end of the road is the Botanical Garden. Enter the Garden ($1 admission). The garden began in the 1920s, when Wrigley's wife Ada began planting native and exotic plants in Avalon Canyon. More recently the garden has greatly expanded and emphasizes native Southern California flora. Particularly interesting are plants endemic to Catalina, including Catalina mahogany, Catalina manzanita, Catalina live-forever, and Catalina ironwood. Pay close attention to the plant identification placards beside the plants; you'll be "tested" on your botany later on the hike.

When you've memorized at least three native plant species, proceed up the dirt path to the Wrigley Memorial. At one time, Wrigley's body was entombed here. If you wish, climb up the many stairs to the 232-foot-wide, 130-foot-high monument, and enjoy the great view of Avalon Harbor.

At this point, intrepid hikers will not proceed back to Avalon for some liquid refreshment, but pass through an unlocked gate below and to the right of the memorial and stride up Memorial Road. Scrub oak, manzanita and lemonade berry—and many more of the same plants, sans identification plaques, that you studied at the Botanic Garden—line the fire road.

The vigorous ascent on Memorial Road offers better and better views of Avalon Harbor. It's likely your approach will flush a covey or two of quail from the brush. Practiced birders might recognize the Catalina quail, a slightly larger and slightly darker subspecies than its mainland relatives.

Memorial Road reaches a divide where, appropriately enough, you'll intersect Divide Road. Bear right. From the 1,000-foot high divide, you'll have commanding views of both sides of the island and of the mainland. The mainland sometimes has an interesting look from this vantage point. The major topographical features of the Southern California basin— the Santa Monica and San Gabriel mountains— are visible, but there is not a trace of civilization!

Continue along the divide, which bristles with prickly pear cactus. The slopes below are crisscrossed with trails made by the island's many wild goats. After about 3/4 of a mile of walking atop the divide, you'll bear right on unsigned Hermit Gulch Trail. This trail is difficult to spot and the early going steep. The trail descends 2.4 miles along a waterless canyon back to Avalon Canyon Road. You'll intersect Avalon Canyon Road a few hundred yards below the Botanical Garden. Turn left and saunter downhill to the comforts of Avalon.

 **15**

Black Jack Trail

8 miles one way: 1,500-foot elevation loss

Catalina Island's terrain is very rugged and bold, characterized by abrupt ridges and V-shaped canyons. Many of the mountaintops are rounded, however, and the western end of this island is grassland and brush, dotted with cactus and seasonal wildflowers. Bison, deer, boar, and rabbits roam the savannas.

This walk is a good introduction to the island; it samples a variety of terrain on the island, inland and coastal. Transportation logistics are a bit complex, but the trail is easy to follow.

Directions to trailhead: For information about ferry service to the island and backcountry visitor permits, consult Walk #14.

From Avalon, you'll be traveling to the trailhead via the Catalina Island Interior Shuttle Bus, which departs from 213 Catalina Avenue (the island's "Main Street") The shuttle bus (fee) will drop passengers off at Black Jack Junction.

The Walk: At signed Black Jack Junction, there's a fire phone and good views of the precipitous west ridges. The trail, a rough fire road, ascends for one mile over brush and cactus-covered slopes. You'll pass the fenced, but open shaft of the old Black Jack Mine (lead, zinc and silver). On your left a road appears that leads up to Black Jack Mountain, at 2,006 feet, the second-highest peak on Catalina. Continue past this junction.

Ahead is a picnic ramada with a large sunshade and nearby a signed junction. You may descend to Black Jack Camp, which is operated by Los Angeles County. Here you'll find tables, shade, and water. Set in a stand of pine, the camp offers fine channel views.

Bear right on the signed Cottonwood/Black Jack Trail. A second junction soon appears. Continue straight downhill. The other trail ascends to Mt. Orizaba (2,097 feet), the island's highest peak.

The trail descends steeply through a canyon, whose steep walls are a mixture of chaparral and grassland and are favored by a large herd of wild goats. At the bottom of the canyon, pass through three gates of a private ranch. (Close all gates; don't let the horses out.) The trail reaches the main road connecting Little Harbor with Airport-in-the-Sky. You may bear left at this junction and follow the winding road 3 1/2 miles to Little Harbor. For a more scenic route of about the same distance, turn right on the road. Hike about 200 yards to the end of the ranch fence line, then bear left, struggling cross-country briefly through spiney brush and intersect a ranch road. This dirt road follows the periphery of the fence line on the east side of the ranch to the top of a canyon. You bear left again, still along the fence line. You ascend and then descend, staying atop this sharp shadeless ridge above pretty Big Springs Canyon. When you begin descending toward the sea, you'll spot Little Harbor.

Little Harbor is the primary campground and anchorage on the Pacific side of the island. It's a good place to relax while you're waiting for the shuttle bus, or to refresh yourself for the hike through buffalo country to Two Harbors.

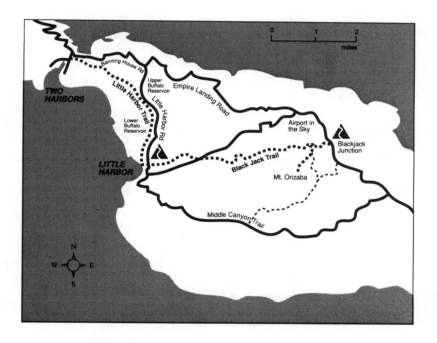

16

Little Harbor Trail

Little Harbor to Two Harbors: 7 miles one way

In 1602, when Vizcaino's ship sailed toward the mountains of Catalina, the explorer was certain he had reached two islands. From a distance, the mountainous land on the east end appears to be separated from a smaller portion on the west end; in fact, it's an optical illusion. The eye is tricked by a low-lying isthmus, the narrowest section of Catalina. Catalina Harbor lies on the ocean side of this isthmus, Isthmus Cove on the channel side, and together this area is called Two Harbors.

As the Wrigley family opened the isle to tourism, Two Harbors pursued a destiny apart from Avalon. In the 1920s and 1930s, it was a peaceful sanctuary for film celebrities and the Los Angeles elite who could indulge in the luxury of yachting.

This walk takes you across the island from the Pacific side to the channel side and offers fine views and a chance to watch buffalo. Your destination is Two Harbors, popular with campers, boaters and fishermen.

For a relaxing weekend backpack, take the trail from Black Jack Junction (See Walk #15), spend the night at Little Harbor Campground, and hike the next day to Two Harbors.

Directions to trailhead: (See Walk #14 for ferry and shuttle bus information.) A shuttle bus takes you across the island from Avalon to Little Harbor in the morning and will pick you up in Two Harbors for your return

Early walker studies beautiful Little Harbor

to Avalon. If you purchased a ferry ticket from the mainland to Avalon, and plan to leave the island from Two Harbors, please inform the ferry company; no additional charge, but the company needs to know. (See page 55 for map.)

The Walk: The route, a fire road, departs from a former stagestop, Little Harbor, now a popular campground and anchorage. Join Little Harbor Road, and begin ascending higher and higher into Little Springs Canyon. Buffalo graze both sides of the canyon and two reservoirs have been developed for the animals. In 1924, when Hollywood moviemakers were filming Zane Grey's classic western, "The Vanishing American," 14 head of buffalo were brought to the island for the film. Recapturing the buffalo after filming proved impossible so the beasts were left to roam. The animals adapted well to life on Catalina and quickly multiplied. Today's population is held to 400-500, the ideal number for available pasturage.

At an unsigned junction a mile past Lower Buffalo Reservoir, bear left on Banning House Road, which will take you 3 1/4 miles to Two Harbors. (Little Harbor Road continues north, then west to Two Harbors if you prefer to stick to this road.) Rough Banning House Road ascends very steeply up a canyon roamed by wild boar. At the windswept head of the canyon you are rewarded with superb views of the twin harbors of Catalina Harbor and Isthmus Cove and can see both the eastern and western fringes of the island.

A steep northeasterly descent brings you to the outskirts of Two Harbors. You'll have no trouble improvising a route past ranchettes and private clubs to the ferry building.

57

17

Eagle Rock Loop Trail

Topanga parking lot to Eagle Rock via Eagle Rock/Eagle Springs Loop:
6 1/2 miles round trip: 800-foot gain
Topanga parking lot to Will Rogers SHP via Eagle Rock, Fire Road 30,
Rogers Rd.: 10 1/2 miles one way; 1,800-foot loss

For many years hikers have promoted the idea of a 55-mile Backbone Trail following the crest of the Santa Monica Mountains from Will Rogers State Historic Park to Point Mugu State Park. When completed, the trail will link the three large state parks of Topanga, Malibu Creek and Point Mugu, as well as land owned by the National Park Service, and enable Southland residents to spend days and weekends hiking, backpacking and horseback riding along the spine of the Santa Monica Mountains.

From Topanga State Park to Will Rogers State Historic Park, the Backbone Trail has been finished for quite some time and has proved very popular. The lower reaches of the trail offer a fine tour of the wild side of Topanga Canyon while the ridgetop sections offer far-reaching inland and ocean views.

The name Topanga is from the Shoshonean Indian dialect. These Indians and their ancestors occupied the canyon on and off for several thousand years B.C. until the Spanish evicted them and forced them to settle at the San Fernando Mission.

This walk departs from quiet and imperturbable Topanga Canyon, surrounded by Los Angeles sprawl but retaining its rural character. Most of the trail is on good fire road. A longer one-way option takes you along brushy ridges to Will Rogers State Park. On a blustery winter day, city and canyon views are superb.

Directions to trailhead: From Topanga Canyon Boulevard, turn east on Entrada Road; that's to the right if you're coming from Pacific Coast Highway. Follow Entrada Road by turning left at every opportunity until you arrive at Topanga State Park. The trailhead is at the end of the parking lot. There is a park day use fee.

To Will Rogers State Historic Park trailhead: If you're taking the longer hike and want to be met (or leave your car) at Will Rogers State Historic Park, here are the directions to that destination: From Sunset Boulevard in Pacific Palisades, turn north at the park entrance. The road leads up to Rogers' estate, now a state historic park that interprets the cowboy/comedian/ philosopher's life. Near Rogers' home, a signed trail climbs to Inspiration

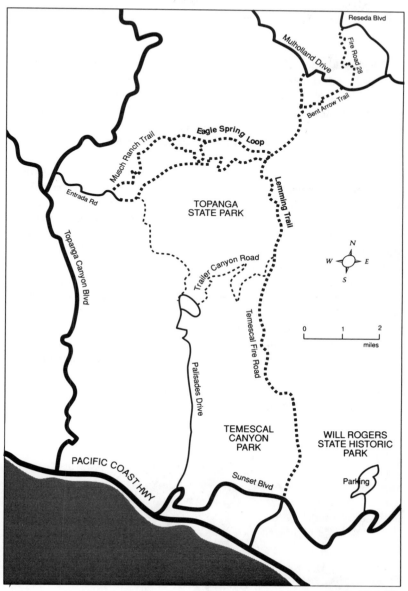

Reseda Blvd

Mulholland Drive

Fire Road 28

Bent Arrow Trail

Musch Ranch Trail

Eagle Spring Loop

Entrada Rd

TOPANGA
STATE PARK

Lemming Trail

Topanga Canyon Blvd

Trailer Canyon Road

N
W   E
S

0   1   2
miles

Palisades Drive

Temescal Fire Road

TEMESCAL
CANYON
PARK

WILL ROGERS
STATE HISTORIC
PARK

PACIFIC COAST HWY

Sunset Blvd

Parking

Trails 17 & 19

Point. Rogers Trail intersects it 1/10th mile past the Inspiration Point Junction.

The Walk: From the Topanga State Park parking lot, follow the distinct trail eastward to a signed junction, where you'll begin hiking on Eagle Springs Road. You'll pass through an oak woodland and through chaparral country. The trail slowly and steadily gains about 800 feet in elevation on the way to Eagle Rock. When you reach a junction, bear left on the north loop of Eagle Springs Road to Eagle Rock. A short detour will bring you to the top of the rock.

To complete the loop, bear sharply right (southwest) at the next junction, following the fire road as it winds down to Eagle Spring. Past the spring, you return to Eagle Spring Road and retrace your steps back to the trailhead.

Three-mile long Musch Ranch Trail, which passes from hot chaparral to shady oak woodland, crosses a bridge and passes the park pond, is another fine way to return to the trailhead.

Option: To Will Rogers State Historic Park. Follow the loop trip directions to the northeast end of Eagle Rock/Eagle Spring Loop, where you bear right on Fire Road 30. In 1/2 mile you reach the intersection with Rogers Road. Turn left and follow the dirt road (really a trail) for 3 1/2 miles, where the road ends and meets Rogers Trail. Here a level area and solitary oak suggest a lunch stop. On clear days, enjoy the spectacular views in every direction: To the left are Rustic Canyon and the crest of the mountains near Mulholland Drive. To the right, Rivas Canyon descends toward the sea.

Stay on Rogers Trail, which marches up and down several steep hills, for about two more miles, until it enters Will Rogers Park near Inspiration Point.

Mounted volunteers patrol Santa Monica Mountains trails

▲ 18
Backbone Trail

Tapia County Park to Castro Crest: 7 miles one way;
2,000-foot elevation gain
Return through Malibu Creek State Park via Bulldog Motorway,
Twentieth Century Road 14 miles round trip:
2,000-foot elevation gain

For many years, hikers have promoted the idea of a 55-mile Backbone Trail following the crest of the Santa Monica Mountains from Will Rogers State Historic Park to Point Mugu State Park. When completed, the trail would link the three large state parks of Topanga, Malibu Creek and Point Mugu, as well as land owned by the National Park Service, and enable Southland residents to spend days and weekends hiking, backpacking and horseback riding along the spine of the Santa Monica Mountains.

The Backbone Trail route through Malibu Creek State Park has been finished for quite some time and has proved very popular. Both a primary and alternate route lead through the state park. The high "primary" route follows a dramatic ridgetop toward Castro Crest while the "alternate" route meanders along with Malibu Creek through the heart of the state park.

This walk connects the two branches of the Backbone Trail and provides a grand tour of Malibu Creek State Park. Fine ocean and island views are offered along the first half of the hike and a chance to explore geologically and ecologically unique Malibu Creek Canyon on the second half.

Directions to trailhead: From Pacific Coast Highway about 20-miles up-coast from Santa Monica, turn inland on Malibu Canyon Road and proceed 5 miles to Tapia County Park, located a short mile south of Malibu Creek State Park.

From the parking lot, return to Malibu Canyon Road and walk south. Using caution, cross the road and walk across the bridge spanning Malibu Creek. Recross the road and walk a few hundred feet to a "35 mph—curve" sign, where the trail begins. Two other signs that provide no useful information to the hiker—"Tractors only" and a state park boundary—are implanted at this ugly trailhead. (Don't judge a book by its cover or a trail by its trailhead; a few hundred yards into this hike, the Backbone Trail becomes much more inspiring.)

The Walk: Mesa Peak Motorway, as this dirt road is known, ascends steeply at first, gaining 1,500 feet in 2 1/2 miles. With the elevation gain

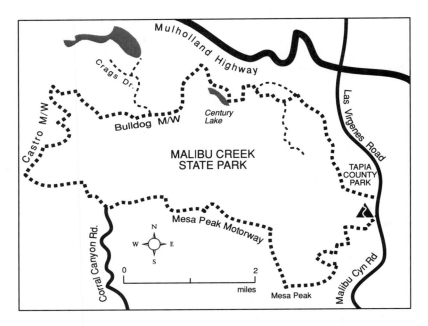

comes sweeping panoramic views of Point Dume, Santa Monica Bay, and Palos Verdes Peninsula. On clear days, Catalina, San Clemente, Anacapa and Santa Cruz Islands float upon the horizon.

The trail veers left toward Mesa Peak (1,844 feet) and continues climbing in a northwesterly direction through an area rich in fossilized shells. Hillside roadcuts betray the Santa Monica Mountains' oceanic heritage. As you hike the spine of the range, a good view to the north is yours: the volcanic rocks of Goat Butte tower above Malibu Creek gorge and the path of Triunfo Canyon can be traced.

The road passes through an area of interesting sandstone formations and intersects paved Corral Canyon Road, which is termed Castro Motorway from this point. Continue west on Castro Motorway for one mile, reaching the intersection with Bulldog Motorway.

The Backbone Trail continues west toward the forest of antennas atop Castro Peak (2,824 feet) and hopefully, someday to Point Mugu.

Option: Return via Bulldog Motorway. For a nice loop trip back through Malibu Creek State Park, bear right on Bulldog Motorway. Descend steeply under transmission lines, veering east and dropping into Triunfo Canyon. In 3 1/2 miles, you reach Twentieth Century Road. Turn right and soon pass what was once the location of the exterior sets used by the M*A*S*H television series. (The set is now on display in the Smithsonian.) The prominent Goat Buttes that tower above Malibu Creek are featured in the opening shot of each episode.

The road passes Century Lake, crosses a ridge, then drops down to Malibu Creek and comes to a fork in the road. Take either the left (high road) or continue straight ahead over the bridge on the low road; the roads meet again downstream, so you may select either one. One-half mile after the roads rejoin, you approach the park's day use parking area.

Follow a dirt road that skirts this parking area, leads past a giant valley oak and approaches the state park's newly constructed (but not yet open) campground.

Bear right on a dirt road that leads a short distance through meadowland to the park's new Group Camp. Here you'll join a connector trail, signed with the international hiking symbol, that will take you a mile up and over a low brushy ridge to Tapia Park. Walk through the park back to your car.

"The Gorge,"
Malibu Creek

19

Lemming Trail

San Fernando Valley to the Sea: 12 miles one way;
2,000-foot elevation gain

You won't find any lemmings along the Southern California coast; the furry, short tailed, mice-like creatures inhabit Arctic not Mediterranean climes. The Lemming Trail takes its name not from the rodent's presence in the Santa Monica Mountains, but from its proclivity to rush headlong into the sea.

A crisp cool winter or spring day is a great time to make like a lemming and hike from the San Fernando Valley to the sea. The Lemming Trail offers a grand tour of the Santa Monica Mountains, the only relatively undeveloped mountain range in the U.S. that bisects a major metropolitan area. You'll travel from Tarzana to Topanga to Temscal to the Pacific on a network of trails and fire roads and be treated to some superb coastal vistas.

Though the Lemming Trail was named for a small rodent, be assured that this is no Mickey Mouse hike. Be prepared for a very long and strenuous day.

Directions to trailhead: (See page 59 for map) This is a one-way walk so a car shuttle or a helpful non-hiking friend to assist with the transportation logistics is necessary. Leave one car at Will Rogers State Beach (fee) or along Pacific Coast Highway (free) near the intersection of the Coast Highway and Temescal Canyon Road. Next proceed up coast on PCH to Topanga Canyon Road (27) and drive inland through the canyon to Ventura Boulevard. Turn right (east) and head into Tarzana. Turn right on Reseda Boulevard and follow this road to its end. (A quick route to the Lemming trailhead is to exit the Ventura Freeway (101) on Reseda Boulevard and drive east to its end.)

The Walk: Descend to the dirt road (Fire Road 28) that meanders up the bottom of Caballero Canyon. The sycamore-dotted canyon bottom hosts an intermittent stream. After a mile, the fire road veers left and climbs to a locked gate on Mulholland Drive.

Turn right onto Mulholland and after walking a half-mile, look leftward for the Bent Arrow Trail, which will take you into Topanga State Park. Follow this trail, which at first parallels Mulholland, for a half-mile as it contours around a steep slope and reaches Temescal Fire Road (Fire Road 30). Turn left and begin a moderate descent. After a mile and a half, you'll pass junctions with fire roads on your right leading to Eagle Rock and Eagle

Spring. Continue straight ahead past these junctions on the sharp ridgeline separating Santa Ynez and Temescal Canyons. You'll pass the junction with Rogers Road which leads to Will Rogers State Historic Park. Near the intersection of Rogers Road and Temescal Fire Road is Temescal Peak (2,126 feet), highest peak in Topanga State Park. If you wish, scramble up a short and steep firebreak to the top for a fine view.

After one and a half miles of mostly level walking beyond the Rogers Road intersection, you'll pass Trailer Canyon Road and a mile farther south, Split Rock Road. A microwave tower, atop what locals have dubbed "Radio Peak," stands halfway between the points.

As you descend along the ridge, you'll see some rock outcroppings. A short side trip off the fire road will bring you to Skull Rock, where you can climb inside the wind-formed (aeolian) caves to cool off or picnic. From the ridgetop, the view to the southwest down at the housing developments isn't too inspiring, but the view of the rough unaltered northern part of Temescal Canyon is superb.

As you sweat it out crossing the exposed ridge, you might be amused to learn that "temescal" is what the Chumash Indians called their village sweathouse. The Chumash took as many as two ceremonial sweat baths a day, in what anthropologists speculate might have been a religious ritual. Mission fathers complained that the Chumash took too many baths and were a little too clean. More work at the mission and less relaxation in the sweathouse would be more productive, the padres thought.

Temescal Fire Road narrows and switchbacks down into Temescal Canyon. You might want to stop and cool off at the small waterfall here at the Temescal Creek crossing at the bottom of the canyon. Your route crosses over to the east side of the canyon and descends the canyon bottom on a trail shaded by oaks, willows, and sycamores.

You'll join a paved road and walk through the Presbyterian Conference Center, then join paved Temescal Canyon Road—or improvise a parallel route down canyon through a small park managed by the Santa Monica Mountains Conservancy.

After crossing Sunset Boulevard, you'll walk an easy mile through Temescal Canyon City Park to Pacific Coast Highway. Across Coast Highway is Will Rogers State Beach. Local mountaineering tradition dictates that you emulate the lemming and rush into the sea.

▲ 20
Zuma Dume Trail

Zuma Beach to Pt. Dume: 1 mile round trip
Zuma Beach to Paradise Cove: 3 miles round trip

Zuma Beach is one of Los Angeles County's largest sand beaches and one of the finest white sand strands in California. Zuma lies on the open coast beyond Santa Monica Bay and thus receives heavy breakers crashing in from the north. From sunrise to sunset, board and body surfers try to catch a big one. Every month the color of the ocean and the Santa Monica Mountains seem to take on different shades of green, depending on the season and sunlight, providing the Zuma Beach walker with yet another attraction.

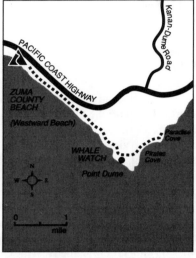

During the whale watching season (approximately mid-December through March), walkers ascending to the lookout atop Point Dume have a good chance of spotting a migrating California gray whale. National Park rangers are often on hand to help you sight the whales.

This walk travels along that part of Zuma Beach known as Westward Beach, climbs over the geologically fascinating Pt. Dume Headlands for sweeping views of the coast, then descends to Paradise Cove, site of a romantic little beach and a fishing pier.

Directions to trailhead: From Pacific Coast Highway, about 25 miles up-coast from Santa Monica and just down-coast from Zuma Beach County Park, turn oceanward on Westward Beach Road and follow it to its end at a parking lot. There is a an entrance fee.

Consult a tide table. Passage is easier at low tide.

The Walk: Proceed down-coast along sandy Westward Beach. You'll soon see a distinct path leading up the point. The trail ascends through a plant community of sea fig, sage, coreopsis and prickly pear cactus to a lookout point.

66

Watch for migrating California gray whales from the Point Dume lookout

During the winter months, the possibility of spotting a migrating gray whale swimming south toward Baja is good. The migration route brings them quite close to shore.

From atop Point Dume, you can look down at Pirate's Cove, two hundred yards of beach tucked away between two rocky outcroppings. In past years this beach was the scene of much dispute between nude beach advocates, residents and the county sheriff.

As you stand atop the rocky triangle projecting into the Pacific, observe the dense black Zuma volcanics and the much softer white sedimentary beds of the sea cliffs extending both east and west. The volcanics have resisted the crashing sea far better than the sedimentary rock and have protected the land behind from further erosion, thus forming the triangle shape of the point.

From the lookout, retrace your steps a short distance and continue on the main trail over the point, which has been set aside as a preserve under the protection of the California Department of Fish and Game. A staircase lets you descend to the beach.

A mile of beach walking brings you to Paradise Cove, sometimes called Dume Cove. It's a secluded spot, and the scene of much television and motion picture filming. The Sand Castle restaurant and a private pier are located at the cove.

21

Leo Carrillo Beach Trail

Leo Carrillo State Beach to County line: 3 miles round trip

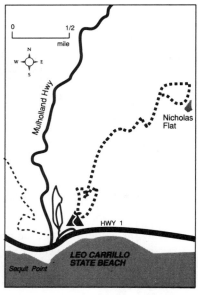

The state beach is named after Angeline Leo Carrillo, famous for his TV role as Cisco Kid's sidekick. Carrillo was also quite active in recreation and civic matters.

Leo Carrillo State Beach is stabilized to some extent by minor rocky breaks in the shoreline and by extensive kelp beds offshore. Seals sometimes come ashore. (Don't disturb.) The beach is a popular locale for moviemakers, and after the propmaster installs palm trees the beach doubles for a South Seas locale.

The trail follows one of L.A.'s more interesting and natural beaches. At Sequit Point you'll find good surfing, swimming, skin diving and a cluster of caves and coves.

Inland areas of Leo Carrillo State Park are also fun to explore by trail. Three-mile long Yellow Hill Trail climbs Arroyo Sequit Ridge for panoramic views of the coast and Channel Islands. Four-mile long Nicholas Flat Trail visits a pond and offers fine spring wildflower displays

Directions to trailhead: Leo Carrillo State Beach is located just downcoast from Mulholland Highway on Pacific Coast Highway near the Los Angeles/Ventura county line. Park along PCH (free) or the state beach (fee).

The Walk: Head up-coast toward Sequit Point. The point bisects the beach, forming a bay to the south. Surfers tackle the well-shaped south swell, battling the submerged rocks and kelp beds.

As you near the point, you'll pass a path which leads under the highway and connects the beach with the sycamore-shaded campground. The state got a bit carried away with pouring asphalt at Leo Carrillo, but it's still a nice park. Scramble around the rocks of Sequit Point to several rock formations, caves, coves, a rock arch and some nice tidepools.

Leo Carrillo State Beach

North of the point, Leo Carrillo Beach offers good swimming with a sandy bottom. The unspoiled coast here is contrasted with development in the county line area. When the beach narrows and the houses multiply, return the same way.

# 22
Overlook Trail

Loop from Sycamore Canyon Trailhead: 10 miles round trip;
1,300-foot gain

Overlook Trail is a fine way to explore the autumn delights of Point Mugu State Park, the largest preserved area in the Santa Monica Mountains. The trail offers fine views of the coast and Channel Islands, and by returning via Sycamore Canyon you can see the park's handsome sycamores cloaked in their fall colors.

Fall is the season when millions of monarch butterflies arrive in the coastal woodlands of Central and Southern California. The monarch's awe-inspiring migration and formation of what entomologists call over-wintering colonies are two of nature's most colorful autumn events.

All monarch butterflies west of the Rockies head for California in the fall; one of the best places in Southern California to observe the arriving monarchs is near the campground in Big Sycamore Canyon at Point Mugu State Park.

During October and November, Sycamore Canyon offers the twin delights of falling autumn leaves and fluttering butterflies. Ask park rangers where the butterflies cluster in large numbers.

Directions to trailhead: From Santa Monica, drive up-coast on Highway 1, for thirty-two miles to the Big Sycamore Canyon Campground in Point Mugu State Park. Outside the campground entrance, there's a dirt area where you may park. Walk past the campground entrance through the campground to a locked gate. The trail (a fire road) begins on the other side of the gate.

The Walk: Follow the path up-canyon along the seasonal creek. Underground water keeps much of the creekside vegetation green year-round.

One-half mile from the the campground, you'll spot the signed Overlook Trail. Bear left and follow the wide trail, which climbs steadily to the sharp ridge that separates Big Sycamore Canyon and La Jolla Canyon. From the ridge you can look down at the ocean and a sandy beach. Listen carefully and you can hear the distant booming of the surf.

The Overlook Trail turns north and continues climbing. To your right, you'll get an aviator's view of Big Sycamore Canyon. Three miles from the trailhead, you'll see La Jolla Canyon below and to the west of the ridge you've been following. Mugu Peak, Laguna Peak with its missile tracking

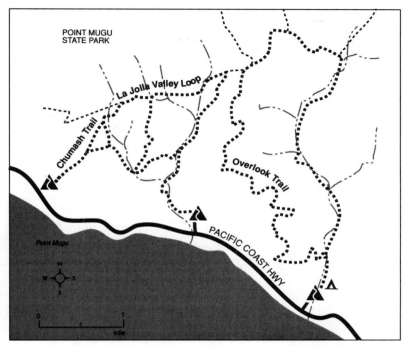

Trails 22, 23 & 24

equipment, and La Jolla Peak tower above La Jolla Valley.

Overlook Trail ends at a signed junction and you will bear right on a dirt road, known as Pumphouse Trail, and descend somewhat steeply to Deer Camp Junction. Drinking water and picnic tables under the shade of oak trees, suggest a lunch stop here.

From Deer Camp Junction, you'll descend 3/4 mile on Wood Canyon Trail to Wood Canyon Junction, the hub of six trails leading to all corners of the park. If you have a trails map, this is a good place to orient yourself and perhaps plan future outings in the state park.

This walk joins the signed Big Sycamore Canyon Trail and heads south (down-canyon) for four gentle miles through one of California's finest sycamore savannas back to the trailhead. Don't let the large and cranky blue jay population discourage you from dawdling under the magnificent sycamores.

71

23

La Jolla Valley Loop Trail

7 miles round trip: 700-foot gain

Ringed by ridges, the native grassland of La Jolla Valley welcomes the walker with its drifts of oak and peaceful pond. This pastoral upland in the heart of Point Mugu State Park is unique: it has resisted the invasion of non-native vegetation. It's rare to find native grassland in Southern California because the Spanish introduced oats and a host of other foreign grasses for pasture for their cattle. In most cases, the imported grasses squeezed out the natives, but not in La Jolla Valley.

La Jolla Valley Loop Trail passes a small waterfall and tours the beautiful grasslands of the valley. This is a fine pathway to follow during the spring when wildflowers and numerous coastal shrubs are in bloom. This is a trail that smells as good as it looks.

Directions to trailhead: Drive about 30 miles up the coast on Pacific Coast Highway from Santa Monica (21 miles up from Malibu Canyon Road if you're coming from the Ventura Freeway and the San Fernando Valley). The turnoff is 1.5 miles north of Big Sycamore Canyon Trailhead, which is also part of Point Mugu State Park. From the turnoff, bear right to the parking area. The signed trailhead, near an interpretive display, is at a fire road that leads into the canyon.

In 1986, the trailhead was named the Ray Miller Trailhead, a tribute to volunteer ranger Ray Miller who is stationed at the trailhead that now bears his name.

The Walk: The fire road leads north up the canyon along the stream bed. As the canyon narrows, some tiny waterfalls come into view. Past the falls, the trail passes some giant coreopsis plants. In early spring the coreopsis, also known as the tree sunflower, sprouts large blossoms. Springtime travel on this trail takes the hiker past the dainty blue and white blossoms of the ceanothus and the snowy white blossoms of the chamise. Pause to take in the sight (and pungent smell!) of the black sage with its light-blue flowers and hummingbird sage with its crimson flowers.

At the first trail junction, bear right on the La Jolla Valley Loop Trail. In a little less than a half-mile, you'll arrive at another junction. Leave the main trail and you will descend the short distance to a lovely cattail pond. The pond is a nesting place for a variety of birds including the redwing blackbird. Ducks and coots paddle the perimeter.

Returning to the main trail, you'll skirt the east end of La Jolla Valley, enjoy an overview of waving grasses and intersect a "T" junction. To the right .7 mile away, is Deer Camp Junction, which provides access to trails leading to Sycamore Canyon and numerous other destinations in the state park. Bear left and in half a mile you'll arrive at La Jolla Valley Camp. The camp, sheltered by oaks and equipped with piped water and tables, is an ideal picnic spot. The valley is a nice place to spend a day. You can snooze in the sun, watch for deer, or perhaps stalk the rare and elusive chocolate lily, known as the Cleopatra of the lily family— the darkest and the loveliest.

After leaving the camp, you could turn left on a short connector trail that skirts the pond and takes you back to La Jolla Valley Loop Trail, where you retrace your steps on that trail and La Jolla Canyon Trail.

To complete the circle on La Jolla Valley Loop Trail, however, continue a half-mile past the campground to the signed junction where you'll bear left and follow a connector trail back to La Jolla Canyon Trail. (See page 71 for map.)

La Jolla Valley Pond

73

▲ 24
Chumash Trail

Coast Highway to Mugu Peak: 3 miles round trip; 1,000-foot gain

Indian trails rarely contoured or switchbacked up a slope; they headed directly up them. Chumash Trail, a typical Indian trail, ascends vigorously straight up the steep shoulders of Mugu Peak.

Chumash Trail honors the native people who lived for many, many centuries on the land we now call Pt. Mugu State Park. This trail connected the rich tidelands with the gentle La Jolla Valley area, which was dotted with Chumash villages. Muwu meant "beach," and the Chumash Trail is littered with seashells.

This walk climbs to Mugu Peak which, along with Laguna Peak and La Jolla Peak, anchor the western end of the Santa Monica Mountains. From atop the peak, the walker is treated to views of the Pacific, Channel Islands and Mugu Lagoon.

Directions to trailhead: Drive about thirty miles up-coast from Santa Monica, two miles up-coast from the La Jolla Canyon trailhead, and park on the inland side of Pacific Coast Highway in a large turnout just opposite the Seabee rifle range.

The Walk: The trail ascends enthusiastically uphill to the east over prickly pear cactus and coreopsis-covered slopes. Three-quarters of a mile of climbing brings you to an unmarked junction with a trail that contours around Mugu Peak; this path will be your return route from the peak.

Continuing north, you'll briefly join La Jolla Valley Loop Trail and arrive at a saddle. (La Jolla Valley Loop Trail continues to the native tall grass prairie in the valley and connects with several other park trails. See Walk #23) Look sharply eastward for an unsigned path that ascends to the peak. Enjoy the ocean views and the panorama of La Jolla Valley.

From the summit of Mugu Peak, join the path that descends southeast to an old road that circles the peak. Bear right on this path, which contours first west then north around the peak and returns you to Chumash Trail and in turn, to the trailhead. (See page 71 for map.)

View of Mugu Lagoon from Mugu Peak

25

Mcgrath Beach Trail

McGrath State Beach to McGrath Lake: 4 miles round trip
McGrath State Beach to Oxnard Shores: 8 miles round trip
McGrath State Beach to Channel Islands Harbor: 12 miles round trip

McGrath State Beach and McGrath Lake were named for the McGrath family which had extensive land holdings in the area dating from 1874. Located on the western city limits of Oxnard, the 2-mile long state beach extends south from the Santa Clara River.

A small lake in the southern portion of the park helps to attract more than two hundred species of birds, including white-tailed kites, marsh hawks, owls, and herons. Such rare birds as ospreys, white wagtails and black skimmers have been sighted here. The Santa Clara Estuary Natural Preserve on the northern boundary of the park also offers a haven for birds and habitat for weasels, skunks, jackrabbits, opossum, squirrels and mice, plus tortoises and gopher snakes.

Near the state beach entry kiosk, a small visitors center has exhibits about the areas plant and wildlife.

This walk takes you on a nature trail through the Santa Clara River Estuary, visits McGrath Lake and travels miles of sandy beach to Channel Islands Harbor.

Directions to trailhead: To reach McGrath State Beach, visitors southbound on U.S. 101 should take the Seaward Avenue offramp to Harbor Boulevard, turn south on Harbor and travel 3/4 mile to the park. Northbound visitors should exit Highway 101 on Victoria Avenue, turn left at the light, Olivas Park Drive, then right to Harbor Boulevard. Turn left on Harbor and proceed 3/4 mile to the park. The signed nature trail leaves from the day use parking lot. Signposts along the nature trail are keyed to pamphlet, available from the entry kiosk. There is a state park day use fee.

The Walk: From the parking lot, follow the nature trail through the estuary. The river bank is a mass of lush vegetation: willow, silverweed and yerba mansa. In 1980, the Santa Clara River area was declared a natural preserve, primarily to protect the habitat of two endangered species of birds—the California least tern and Belding's Savannah Sparrow.

When you reach nature trail signpost 11, join a nearby trail that leads atop an old levee, first along the river, then down-coast along the periphery of the state beach campground. This trail joins a dirt road and continues down-coast, but the far more aesthetic route is along water's edge, so trudge over the low dunes and walk along the shoreline.

Along the beach, visitors enjoy sunbathing or surf fishing for bass, corbina, or perch. In two miles you'll spot McGrath Lake, tucked away behind some dunes.

As you continue south, more sandy beach and dunes follow. You pass a huge old Edison power plant, and arrive at Oxnard Shores, a development famous for getting clobbered by heavy surf at high tide. The beach is flat and at one time was eroding at the phenomenal rate of ten feet a year. Homes were built right on the shoreline and many have been heavily damaged. New homes are built on pilings, so waves crash under, rather than through them.

Past Oxnard Shores, a mile of beach walking brings you to historic Hollywood Beach. "The Sheik," starring that great silent movie idol Rudolph Valentino, was filmed on the desert-like sands here. Real estate promoters of the time attempted to capitalize on Oxnard Beach's instant fame and re-named it Hollywood Beach. They laid out subdivisions called Hollywood-by-the-Sea and Silver Strand, suggesting to their customers that the area was really a movie colony and might become a future Hollywood.

This walk ends another mile down-coast at the entrance to Channel Islands Harbor.

26

Anacapa Island Loop Trail

2 miles round trip

The Channel Islands beckon not with South Seas or Caribbean sensuousness, but with dramatic mountaintops and jagged shorelines. The only disappointed visitors are casual tourists who, while motoring along U.S. 101, see the sign: Channel Islands National Park. They exit the freeway, only to find that the "national park" on Ventura Harbor is just a reception building. The real park is in the Pacific, 14 to 60 miles away—a series of blue-tinged mountains floating on the horizon.

The islands parallel the Southern California coast, which at this point runs more or less east-west to Point Conception. In 1980, five of eight Channel Islands— Anacapa, San Miguel, Santa Barbara, Santa Cruz and Santa Rosa—became the nation's 40th and Southern California's first national park.

Anacapa Island, closest to the mainland, was called Las Mesitas (Little Tables) by Spanish explorer Gaspar de Portola in 1769. Ventura sheep men once owned the island, which has no water. It's hard to imagine how the sheep survived. The popular belief is that night fog was so dense that the sheep's coats became soaked, each sheep becoming a woolly sponge by morning. Or so the story goes...

Anacapa, 12 miles southwest of Port Hueneme, is the most accessible Channel Island. It offers the walker a sampling of the charms of the larger islands to the west. Below the tall wind-and-wave-cut cliffs, sea lions bark

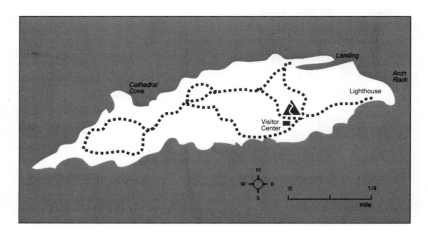

at the crashing breakers. Gulls, owls, herons and pelicans call the cliffs home.

Anacapa is really three islands chained together with reefs that rise above the surface during low tide. West Anacapa is the largest segment, featuring great caves where the Chumash Indians are said to have collected water dripping from the ceiling. The middle isle hosts a wind-battered eucalyptus grove.

The east isle, where the National Park has a visitors center, is the light of the Channel Islands; a Coast Guard lighthouse and foghorn warns ships of the dangerous channel.

This walk tours East Anacapa Island. The island is barely a mile long and a quarter-mile wide, so even though you tour the whole island, it's a short hike.

Directions to trailhead: For the most up-to-date information on boat departures, contact Channel Islands National Park on Ventura Harbor: (805) 644-8157. The park headquarters/visitors center is well worth a visit.

Most commercial tour operators leave from the Ventura and Oxnard

Arch Rock, Anacapa Island

marinas. A number of whale-watching tours are offered during winter when the gray whales migrate. Some of these tour boats land on Anacapa and some don't. One company, Island Packers, runs year-round to Anacapa. Their boats leave every Saturday and Sunday. Weekday trips are scheduled during whale season and in summer. For information, call: (805) 642-1393 or (805) 642-7688.

The Walk: It's a romantic approach to East Anacapa as you sail past Arch Rock. As you come closer, however, the island looks forsaken; not a tree in sight. But as you near the mooring at the east end of the isle, the honeycomb of caves and coves is intriguing. A skiff brings you to the foot of an iron stairway. You climb 150 stairs, ascending steep igneous rocks to the cliff tops.

What you find on top depends on the time of year. In February and March, you may enjoy the sight of 30-ton gray whales passing south on their way to calving and mating waters off Baja California. In early spring, the giant coreopsis, the island's featured attraction, is something to behold. It is called the tree sunflower, an awkward thick- trunked perennial that grows as tall as 10 feet.

The nature trail leaves from the visitors center, where you can learn about island life, past and present. A helpful pamphlet is available describing the island's features. Remember to stay on the trail; the island's ground cover is easily damaged.

Along the trail, a campground and several inspiring cliff-edge nooks invite you to picnic. The trail loops in a figure-eight through the coreopsis and returns to the visitors center.

Anacapa Island

27

San Miguel Island Trail

Cuyler Harbor to Lester Ranch: 3 miles round trip; 700-foot gain

San Miguel is the westernmost of the Channel Islands. Eight miles long, four miles wide, it rises as a plateau, 400 to 500 feet above the sea. Wind-driven sands cover many of the hills which were severely overgrazed by sheep during the island's ranching days. Once owned by the U.S. Navy which used it as a bombing site and missile tracking station, San Miguel is now managed by the National Park Service.

Three species of cormorants, storm petrels, Cassin's auklets, and pigeon guillemot nest on the island. San Miguel is home to six pinniped species: California sea lion, northern elephant seal, steller sea lion, harbor seal, northern fur seal and Guadalupe fur seal. The island may host the largest elephant seal population on earth. As many as 15,000 seals and sea lions can be seen basking on the rocks during mating season.

A trail runs most of the way from Cuyler Harbor to the west end of the island at Point Bennett, where the pinniped population is centered. The trail passes two round peaks, San Miguel and Green Mountain, and drops in and out of steep canyons to view the lunar landscape of the caliche forest. Please check in with the resident ranger and stay on established trails because the island's vegetation is fragile.

Directions to trailhead: Plan a very long day—or better yet, an overnight trip to San Miguel. It's at least a five-hour boat trip from Ventura. There are no regularly scheduled trips to the island. The Cabrillo Marine Museum in San Pedro and the Santa Barbara Natural History Museum sometimes sponsor trips. Contact Island Packers Company at (805) 642-1393 or Channel Islands National Park Headquarters (on Ventura Harbor), 169 Anchors Way Drive, Ventura, CA 93003; (805) 644-8157.

The Walk: Follow the beach at Cuyler Harbor to the east. The harbor was named after the original government surveyor in the 1850s. The beach around the anchorage was formed by a bight of volcanic cliffs that extend to bold and precipitous Harris Point, the most prominent landmark on San Miguel's coast.

At the east end of the beach, about 3/4 of a mile from anchoring waters, a small footpath winds its way up the bluffs. It's a relatively steep trail following along the edge of a stream-cut canyon. At the top of the canyon, the trail veers east and forks. The left fork takes you a short distance to

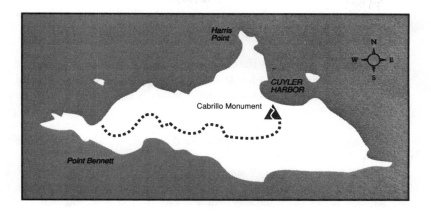

Cabrillo Monument.

Juan Rodriguez Cabrillo, the Portuguese explorer, visited and wrote about San Miguel in October, 1542. While on the island, he fell and broke either an arm or a leg (historians are unsure about this). As a result of this injury he contracted gangrene and died on the island in January, 1543 and it's believed (historians disagree about this, too) he was buried here. In honor of Cabrillo, a monument was erected in 1937.

The right fork continues to the remains of a ranch house. Of the various ranchers and ranch managers to live on the island, the most well-known were the Lesters. They spent twelve years on the island, and their adventures were occasionally chronicled by the local press. When the Navy evicted the Lesters from the island in 1942, Mr. Lester went to a hill overlooking Harris Point, in his view the prettiest part of the island, and shot himself. Within a month his family moved back to the mainland. Not much is left of the ranch now. The buildings burned down in the 1960s, and only a rubble of brick and scattered household items remain.

For a longer 8-mile round trip the hiker can continue on the trail past the ranch to the top of San Miguel Peak (916 feet), down, and then up again to the top of Green Mountain (850 feet). Ask rangers to tell you about the caliche forest, composed of calcified sheaths of plants that died thousands of years ago. Calcium carbonate has reacted with ancient plants' organic acid, creating a ghostly forest.

28

Summerland Trail

Lookout County Park to Biltmore Beach: 5 miles round trip

One might guess Summerland was named for the weather, but the name was taken from Spiritualist literature—something to do with the Second Heaven of Spiritualism. A century ago, Spiritualists pitched their tents on the tiny lots in the area.

In the waters here, the first offshore oil platform in the Western hemisphere was erected in 1896. Soon more than three hundred wells were pumping oil from Pleistocene rocks at depths of 100 to 800 feet, an insignificant depth by today's standards.

Oil attracted far more people to Summerland than Spiritualism, and soon the air was heavy with the smell of gas and oil. It was said that free illumination came easy—one simply pounded a pipe in the ground 'til reaching natural gas, and lit a match. Liberty Hall, the Spiritualists' community center, glowed with divine light and for a time Summerland became known as the White City.

This walk travels due west along sandy Summerland Beach, parts of which are popular with the clothing-optional set, rounds some rocky points, and concludes at the narrow beach in front of the famed Biltmore Hotel.

Directions to trailhead: From Highway 101 in Summerland, take the Summerland exit and turn oceanward to Lookout County Park.

The Walk: At Lookout County Park is a picnic area and a monument commemorating the first offshore oil rig. A well-marked ramp leads to the

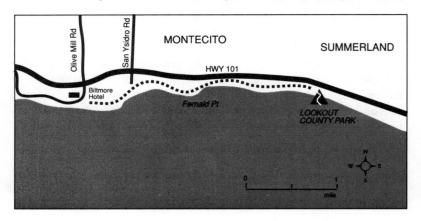

Summerland Beach

beach. From Lookout (Summerland) Beach, a sea wall extends 3/4 mile west to Fernald Point. At high tide, you may wish to walk atop it, but you'll have to battle some brush. You soon pass a pretty little cove, bounded on the far side by Fernald Point, formed by a fan delta deposited at the mouth of Romero Creek.

Around the point, as you approach Montecito, you'll see the higher parts of the Santa Ynez Mountains on the north skyline and the overturned beds of sandstone located near the peaks. There are no official public beaches in Montecito, but most of the shoreline receives public use, Fernald-Sharks Cove is the first beach you travel, then Miramar Beach below the Miramar Hotel. "Miramar-By-the-Sea" has been a popular watering place since the completion of the Southern Pacific railroad line in 1901. The hotel, with its finely landscaped grounds and blue-roofed bungalows, used to be a passenger stop.

In another 1/4 mile, you'll begin hiking across Montecito's third beach, Hammonds, popular with surfers. Hammonds Meadows on the bluffs above the beach is a former Chumash habitation and a potentially rich archaeological dig. Although it was recently placed on the National Register of Historic Places, it's been bulldozed for development.

Up-coast from Hammonds you'll pass a number of fine homes and arrive at narrow Biltmore Beach, frequented by the rich and beautiful. Opposite the beach is the magnificent Biltmore Hotel, built in 1927.

Trails 29 & 30

29

Cold Springs Trail

Mountain Drive to Montecito Overlook: 3 miles round trip;
900-foot gain
Mountain Drive to Montecito Peak: 7 1/2 miles round trip;
2,500-foot gain
Mountain Drive to Camino Cielo: 9 miles round trip;
2,700-foot gain

A few million years ago, the Santa Ynez Mountains rose slowly from the sea. The mountains are not secretive about their origin and display their oceanic heritage in a number of ways. Tilted blocks of sedimentary rock, which have aggregated tens of thousands of feet in thickness, provide the first clue to the mountains' former undersea life. Fossils of sea animals give further testimony that the mountains were once many leagues under the sea.

Santa Ynez Range trails start in lush canyon bottoms, zig-zag up the hot, dry canyon walls, and follow rock ledges to the top of the range. Many of the trails intersect El Camino Cielo (the sky road), which follows the mountain crest. From the top, the walker enjoys sweeping views of the Pacific, Channel Islands and coastal plain.

After the Santa Ynez Forest Reserve was established in 1899, rangers recognized the desirability of a trail crossing the Reserve from coast to desert. A trail up the West Fork of Cold Springs Canyon had historically been the way into the Santa Barbara backcountry, but rangers realized that this tricky trail, which climbed around a waterfall and crossed shale slopes, would be difficult to maintain. In 1905, the Forest Service built a trail up the East Fork of Cold Springs Canyon.

And a lovely trail it is. It begins by the alder- shaded, year-round creek, then rises out of the canyon for fine coastal views.

Directions to trailhead: From Highway 101 in Montecito, a few miles south of Santa Barbara, exit on Hot Springs Road and proceed toward the foothills for 2 1/2 miles to Mountain Drive. Turn left. A mile's travel on Mountain Drive brings you to the Cold Springs trailhead, which begins at a point where a creek flows over a cement drainage apron.

The Walk: The trail immediately crosses the creek to the east side of the canyon. It rises briefly through oak woodland, then returns to the creek. On your left, a quarter-mile from the trailhead, is the easily overlooked, unsigned West Fork Trail. This century-old trail ascends 1 1/2 miles through California bay laurel to Gibraltar Road.

Continuing past the West Fork trail junction, the East Fork Trail rises up the canyon wall and rejoins the creek a half-mile later. Look for a fine swimming hole below you to the right. The trail then switchbacks moderately out of the canyon to Montecito Overlook. Enjoy the view of the Santa Barbara coastline and the Channel Islands.

Past the overlook, you'll cross a fire road leading down to Hot Springs Canyon, begin an uphill climb and soon encounter the Hot Springs connector trail. The one-mile-long connector trail leads down into Hot Springs Canyon. Along the trail thrives bamboo, huge agave, banana and palm trees— remnants of landscaped gardens that surrounded Hot Springs Resort during its glory days. Explore the ruins of Hot Springs Hotel, constructed during the early 1880s. Europeans and Americans from colder climes flocked here to "take the cure." A 1920 fire destroyed the hotel; it was rebuilt and burned again in 1964.

From the junction with the Hot Springs connector trail, Cold Springs Trail switchbacks up canyon and offers fine coastal views. A one-mile climb brings you to two eucalyptus trees (about the only shade en route!) and another 3/4 mile of travel takes you to the unsigned junction with a side trail leading to Montecito Peak (3,214 feet). Enjoy the view and sign the summit register.

Cold Springs Trail continues a last mile to Camino Cielo. From the Sky Road, many trails lead into the far reaches of the Santa Barbara backcountry. Enjoy the grand views and return the same way.

"Our favorite route to the main ridge was by a way called the Cold Springs Trail. We used to enjoy taking visitors up it, mainly because you come on the top suddenly, without warning. Then we collected remarks. Everybody, even the most stolid, said something."

—*Stewart Edward White*
The Mountains, 1906

30

Rattlesnake Canyon Trail

Skofield Park to Tin Can Meadow:
    4 1/2 miles round trip; 1,000-foot gain
Skofield Park to Gibraltar Road
    6 miles round trip; 1,500-foot gain

Rattlesnake Canyon Trail is serpentine, but otherwise far more inviting than its name suggests.

The joys of the canyon were first promoted by none other than the Santa Barbara Chamber of Commerce. Many a turn-of-the-century visitor to Santa Barbara resorts enjoyed hiking and riding in the local mountains. Eager to keep the customers satisfied, in 1902 the chamber purchased easements from canyon homesteaders to develop a recreation trail. "Chamber of Commerce Trail," as the chamber called it, was an immediate success with both tourists and locals. However, to the chamber's consternation, both the trail and the canyon itself continued to be called Rattlesnake. Chamber of Commerce Canyon sounded a bit self-serving, so the chamber tried to compromise with an earlier name, Las Canoas Canyon, and adopted a 1902 resolution to that effect. "The name of Rattlesnake Canyon is unpleasantly suggestive of a reptile," it argued, "which is found no more plentifully there than elsewhere along the mountain range and may deter some nervous persons from visiting that most delightful locality."

In the 1960s, the city of Santa Barbara purchased the canyon as parkland. A handsome wooden sign at the foot of the canyon proudly proclaims: Rattlesnake Canyon Wilderness.

Red-berried toyon, manzanita with its white urn-shaped flowers, and purple hummingbird sage cloak the slopes and offer a variety of smells and textures. In the early spring ceanothus blooms, adding frosty whites and blues to the gray-green thickets. Shooting stars, larkspur, and lupine also spread their color over the slopes and meadows.

Directions to the trailhead: From Highway 101 in Santa Barbara, go uptown (toward the mountains) on State Street to Los Olivos Street. Turn right and proceed a half-mile, passing by the Santa Barbara Mission and joining Mission Canyon Road. Follow this road past its intersection with Foothill Road and make a right on Las Canoas Road. Follow Las Canoas to Skofield Park. Leave your car on the shoulder of the road or in the large parking area near the picnic grounds. The trail begins on Las Canoas Road near the handsome stone bridge that crosses Rattlesnake Creek.

*Mr. and Mrs. Lyman Pope
at Tin Can Shack, 1916*

The Walk: From the sandstone bridge across from Skofield Park, hike up a brief stretch of trail and join a narrow dirt road that parallels the east side of the creek. For lovely picnicking, take any of the steep side trails down to the creek. In the early nineteenth century, the mission padres built a dam in the bottom of the canyon, which channeled water into a stone aqueduct and diverted it into the mission's waterwork system. Portions of the aqueduct still exist and can be see by the careful observer.

The trail zigs and zags across the creek, finally continuing along the west bank to open, grassy Tin Can Meadow. The triangular-shaped meadow gets its name from a homesteader's cabin constructed of chaparral framing and kerosene can shingles and sidings. For the first quarter of this century, Tin Can Shack was an important canyon landmark and several guidebooks of that era mention it. It was a popular destination for picnickers who marveled at the inspired architecture and posed for pictures in front of it. In 1925, a brushfire destroyed the shack, and it soon disintegrated into a pile of tin.

At the apex of the triangular meadow is a junction; a side trail takes you 3/4 mile and climbs 500 feet to its intersection with the Tunnel Trail. To the right, Rattlesnake Canyon Trail climbs about 3/4 of a mile and 500 feet to its intersection with Gibraltar Road. There you will be greeted by an unobstructed view of the South Coast. (See page 86 for map.)

▲ 31
Goleta Beach Trail

Goleta Beach County Park to Coal Oil Point Preserve:
   7 miles round trip
Goleta Beach County Park to Ellwood Oil Field: 12 miles round trip

Around 7:00 on the evening of February 23, 1942, while most Southern Californians were listening to President Roosevelt's fireside chat on the radio, strange explosions were heard near Goleta. In the first (and only) attack on U.S. soil since the War of 1812, a Japanese submarine surfaced off the rich oil field on Ellwood Beach, twelve miles north of Santa Barbara, and lobbed sixteen shells into the tidewater field.

"Their marksmanship was poor," asserted Lawrence Wheeler, proprietor of a roadside inn near the oil fields. Most observers agreed with Wheeler, who added there was no panic among his dinner patrons, "We immediately blacked out the place," he said. "One shell landed about a quarter mile from here and the concussion shook the building, but nobody was scared much."

The unmolested, unhurried Japanese gunners were presumably aiming at the oil installations and the coast highway bridge over the Southern Pacific tracks. Tokyo claimed the raid "a great military success" though the incredibly bad marksmen managed to inflict only $500 worth of damage. The submarine disappeared into the night, leaving behind air raid sirens, a jumpy population and lower real estate values.

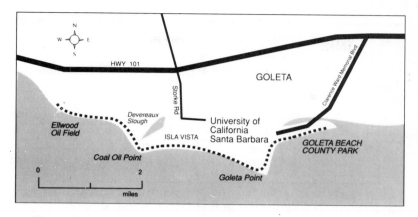

The walk along Goleta Beach to Ellwood Oil Field is interesting for more than historical reasons. On the way to the Oil Field/Battlefield, you'll pass tidepools, shifting sand dunes, and the Devereaux Slough. The slough is a unique intertidal ecosystem, and is protected for teaching and research purposes by Coal Oil Point Preserve.

Directions to trailhead: From Highway 101 in Goleta, head south on Ward Memorial Drive (Route 217) for two miles to Goleta Beach County Park. Park in the large beach lot.

The Walk: Proceed up-coast (west—remember, you're in confusing Santa Barbara County where the coast stretches east to west). In a quarter mile you'll reach a stretch of coast called the Main Campus Reserve Area, where you'll find the Goleta Slough. The same month the Japanese bombed Ellwood Beach, Santa Barbara voters approved a bond issue to buy land around the Goleta Slough and a modern airport was constructed on the site of the old cow pasture/airfield. The slough, host to native and migratory waterfowl, is a remnant of a wetland that was once much more extensive.

Continue up beach past the handsome sandstone cliffs. Occasionally a high tide may force you to detour atop the bluffs through the UC Santa Barbara campus to avoid getting wet. A mile and a half from the county park, you'll round Goleta Point and head due west. You pass a nice tidepool area; judging from the number of college students, it is well studied.

Two more miles of beachcombing brings you to Coal Oil Point. You'll want to explore the nature reserve here. (Please observe all posted warnings; this is a very fragile area.)

The dunes are the first component of the reserve encountered on the seaward side. Sandy hillocks are stabilized with grasses and rushes. Salty sand provides little nourishment, yet the hardy seaside flora manages to survive, settling as close to the water as the restless Pacific will permit. The dunes keep the plants from blowing away and the plants return the favor for the dunes.

Footprints of lizards and mice and miniscule tracks of beetles can be seen tacking this way and that over the sand. The dune's surface records the lightest pressure of the smallest feet. Sometimes one set of animal tracks intersects another in a pattern suggesting the demise of one animal and dinner for another.

Pick up the trail over the dunes on the east side of the reserve. The fennel-lined trail passes under cypress trees and climbs a bluff above the slough to a road on the reserve's perimeter. It's a good place to get "the big picture" of the slough, a unique ecosystem. Something like an estuary, a slough has a mixture of fresh and salt water, but an estuary has a more stable mixture. The water gets quite salty at Devereaux Slough, with little fresh water flushing.

At the slough, birdwatchers rhapsodize over snowy egrets and great blue herons, black bellied plovers and western sandpipers. Avid birdwatchers flock to the slough for birdathons—marathon birdsighting competitions.

In addition to the scores of native and migratory species, birds affection-ately known by their watchers as "vagrants"—lost birds who have no business in the area— often visit the slough. If you're the type who carries a copy of Petersen's Guide in your day pack, you'll spend the rest of the day here and there's no point in urging you to hike on. For the rest of you, it's on to Ellwood.

Option: To Ellwood Oil Field. Return to the beach and continue walking up the coast. Sometimes horses gallop over the dunes, suggesting Peter O'Toole and Omar Sharif's meeting in "Lawrence of Arabia"...except there's oil on the beach, as you'll readily notice when you look at your feet. In two miles you'll pass under an old barnacle-covered oil drilling platform and enter Ellwood Oil Field. Here the Japanese fired shots heard 'round the world...and missed.

32

Gaviota Peak Trail

Highway 101 to Gaviota Peak: 6 miles round trip; 2,000-foot gain

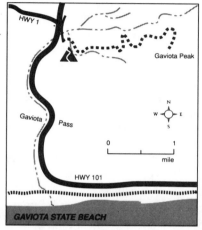

Father Juan Crespi of the 1769 Portola Expedition dubbed the coastline here San Luis, in honor of the King of France. However, the soldiers of the expedition thought that La Gaviota, Spanish for "sea gull," was a more apt description.

This walk begins in Gaviota State Park and ends in Los Padres National Forest. You'll visit warm mineral pools, then continue to the top of Gaviota Peak (2,458 feet) for superb views of the Santa Barbara County coast.

Directions to trailhead: Thirty-five miles up-coast from Santa Barbara, exit Highway 101 at the Lompoc/Highway 1 offramp. Turn east a short distance, then follow the highway frontage road 1/4 mile to the end of the road and park in the Gaviota State Park parking lot.

The Walk: Follow the fire road, which is strewn with rocks and eroded from winter floods. This is a well-used stretch of trail; most folks walk only to the hot springs and turn back. You'll soon leave behind the noise of the highway. A half-mile walk beneath spreading oaks and old sycamores and up a moderate grade brings you to Gaviota Hot Springs.

The springs are more lukewarm than hot. Cross the rock dam, and follow the trail uphill through brush a short distance to a fire road. Bear right.

Walk up the steep fire road, leaving behind the oaks and entering a typical chaparral community. Sometimes this can be a hot hike. During the winter months, however, it can be blustery up here on this ridge route. At times you might be assaulted by clouds, which zoom past, enclosing you in fog for a few seconds.

When you reach the top of the ridge, the trail bears right 1/4 mile to the peak. Atop the peak is a radio relay tower. On clear days, much of the Santa Barbara County coastline, as well as the Channel Islands and Point Conception are visible from Gaviota.

33

Pt. Conception Trail

Jalama County Park to Point Conception: 10 miles round trip

At Point Conception, the western running shoreline of Southern California turns sharply northward and heralds a number of changes: a colder Pacific, foggier days, cooler air. Ecological differences between the north and south coasts are illustrated by the differing marine life occupying the two sections. Point Conception serves as a line of demarcation between differing species of polyps, abalone, crabs and limpets. Climatically, geographically and sociologically, it can be argued that Southern California ends at Point Conception.

This walk takes you along a pristine section of beach and retraces the route of the De Anza Trail, a trail lost to most hikers for over 200 years. The De Anza Trail was the route of Juan Bautista de Anza expedition of 1775-6, which brought 240 colonists from Mexico across the Colorado Desert up the coast to found the city of San Francisco.

Historically, the Anza Trail is much better documented than the Lewis and Clark or other trails that opened up the west. This is due to the meticulous diary-keeping of Anza and the expedition's chaplain, Father Font.

On February 26, 1776, the Anza expedition reached an Indian village called Rancheria Nueva, just east of Pt. Conception. Father Font noted the generosity of the Indians, praised their well-crafted baskets and stone cups and concluded that the Indians would be good recruits for future missions.

This walk leaves from Jalama County Park, the only genuinely public access point between Gaviota State Park and Jalama County Park. You can legally walk along the beach from Jalama County Park to within a half-mile of the Point.

This part of the coast is divided between two huge ranches: the Hollister Ranch, which controls the land between Gaviota State Park and Point Conception and the Bixby Ranch, which occupies the land between Point

96

Conception and Jalama.

Travel writer Frank Riley has facetiously remarked that "Anza, Father Font, Father Junipero Serra and Jesus himself would have to carry bail money to round Point Conception by land today." Riley is right; public outrage will ultimately see to it that some sort of trail or bike path gives the public access to the coast, but in the meantime be warned that the Bixby Ranch and Hollister Ranch are among the most agressively anti-coastal access property holders in the state.

Directions to trailhead: Jalama County Park is located 20 miles southwest of Lompoc off Highway 1. From Highway 101, near Gaviota, exit on Highway 21 north and proceed 14 miles to Jalama Road. Turn left and go 14 miles through some beautiful ranch country to the county park.

The Walk: Before heading south over the splendid sand dunes, check the tide table at the camp store. This walk is best (and sometimes must be) done at low tide. As you walk along the coast, you'll soon realize that although Jalama County Park is not on the main L.A.-San Francisco thoroughfare, two groups have found it and claimed it as their own - surfers and surf fishermen.

Jalama County Park includes only 1/2 mile of shoreline, so you soon walk beyond the park boundary. The sandy beach narrows and gives way to a rockier shore. Offshore, on the rocky reefs, seals linger. They seem to enjoy basking in the sun and getting doused by the breakers. Depending on the tide, you'll encounter a number of sea walls. The smooth tops of the sea walls make a good trail. "1934" is the date imbedded in the concrete walls.

Occasionally, Southern Pacific railroad tracks come into view, though with the crashing of the breakers, you can barely hear the passing trains. Since there are no public roads along this section of the coast, walking or looking out a train window are the only two ways to see this country. Halfway through your walk, after some lazy bends, the coastline heads almost due south and the Pt. Conception Coast Guard Reservation comes into view.

A half-mile from the lighthouse, you'll run out of beach to walk; passage is blocked by waves crashing against a rocky point. Stay away from the lighthouse and Coast Guard Reservation: visitors are not welcome. A blufftop dirt road and a number of cow trails lead toward the lighthouse, established by the federal government in 1855; however, these routes, popular with coast walkers for decades, cross private ranch land.

CENTRAL COAST

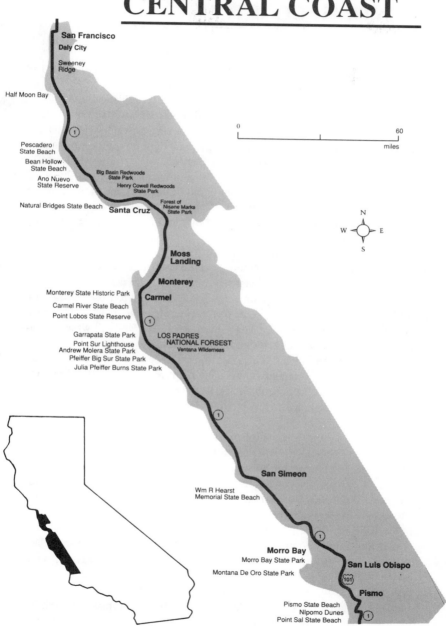

San Francisco
Daly City
Sweeney Ridge

Half Moon Bay

Pescadero State Beach
Bean Hollow State Beach
Ano Nuevo State Reserve

Big Basin Redwoods State Park
Henry Cowell Redwoods State Park

Natural Bridges State Beach

Santa Cruz

Forest of Nisene Marks State Park

Moss Landing

Monterey

Monterey State Historic Park

Carmel

Carmel River State Beach

Point Lobos State Reserve

Garrapata State Park
Point Sur Lighthouse
Andrew Molera State Park
Pfeiffer Big Sur State Park
Julia Pfeiffer Burns State Park

LOS PADRES NATIONAL FORSEST
Ventana Wilderness

San Simeon

Wm R Hearst Memorial State Beach

Morro Bay
Morro Bay State Park

San Luis Obispo

Montana De Oro State Park

Pismo

Pismo State Beach
Nipomo Dunes
Point Sal State Beach

N
W · E
S

0 _____ 60
miles

99

CENTRAL COAST

The coast and coast ranges between Point Conception and Monterey are often lyrically referred to as The Middle Kingdom.

Walkers can explore a hundred miles of San Luis Obispo County Coast, hiking across wide sandy beaches, around protected bays, and over rugged headlands. Bird-watchers gaze at the shimmering tops of eucalyptus trees where great blue herons build their nests, rock hounds gather moonstones, clammers dig for Pismo and razorback clams.

Southern San Luis Obispo County's coastline is dominated by windswept sand dunes, great heaps of sand held in place by ice plant, verbena, grasses, sea rocket and silver lupine. The longshore currents that normally carry sand along the coast is interrupted by rocky headlands; the sand stays in the local area, later to be deposited by the wind on the dunes above the beach.

Morro Bay, and its adjacent mudflats is an amazingly fertile wetland, one of the largest and most significant wildlife habitats on the California coast. The bay ranks within the top ten areas in the nation in terms of numbers of bird species sighted in a single day. Guarding the bay is the much-photographed Morro Rock, "The Gibraltar of the Pacific," which stands halfway between Los Angeles and San Francisco.

North of Morro Bay tall bluffs rise above the beach. Land and sea blend into one astounding tableau. Unlike the theatrical cliffs of Big Sur, these bluffs are accessible; they ebb and flow toward the Coast Highway like the tide, sometimes 20 feet away, sometimes a mile, and always an adventure for coast walkers.

Monterey County's coastline extends from the dramatic Big Sur area to the flat sandy coastal plain along Monterey Bay. Both geographically and spiritually, Big Sur is the heart of California. Trails lead through this heartland across the rugged mountainous terrain of the 159,000-acre Ventana Wilderness. From the windswept ridges of the Santa Lucia Mountains, walkers look down at what is often called, "the greatest meeting of land and sea in the world."

Big Sur country is not a gentle wilderness, but a dramatic, enchanted land. Walkers can explore the Carmel, Little Sur, and Big Sur Rivers, which originate in the Ventana Wilderness. Observant travelers may spot a rare and beautiful spire-like tree, the Santa Lucia fir, which grows only in the Santa Lucia Mountains. In these mountains also is the southernmost limit of the natural range of the coast redwood. Fern-lined canyons, oak-studded

Elephant seals, Ano Nuevo State Reserve

potreros and meadows smothered with Douglas iris, pink owl's clover and California poppies welcome the backcountry adventurer.

At Point Lobos State Reserve, the Monterey cypress makes a last stand. Some of photographer Ansel Adams' greatest work was inspired by the wind-sculpted cypress, lonely sentinels at the edge of the continent.

Before the 1849 gold rush and overnight rise of the city and port of San Francisco, Monterey was the political and commercial center of California. A waterfront walk of Monterey offers a glimpse backwards at this time—and other colorful periods of the city's history. Walkers will enjoy visiting Cannery Row, Fisherman's Wharf and the world- renowned Monterey Bay Aquarium.

North of Monterey Bay are the state redwood parks of the Santa Cruz Mountains and the dramatic coastline of San Mateo County. At Ano Nuevo State Reserve, you'll be treated to a wildlife drama that attracts visitors from all over the world—a close-up look at the largest mainland population of elephant seals.

For centuries, San Francisco Bay's infamous fog and its narrow opening concealed the bay from passing ships. But a coast walker—Captain Gaspar de Portola—sighted it on November 4, 1769. The actual discovery site is atop Sweeney Ridge above the town of Pacifica.

Walking the central coast gives you the chance to re-live the state's colorful history, and make a few discoveries of your own.

 **34**

Point Sal Trail

Point Sal State Beach to Point Sal: 5 miles round trip

When your eye travels down a map of the south/central California coast, you pause on old and familiar friends—the state beaches at San Simeon, Morro Bay, and Pismo Beach. Usually overlooked is another state beach— remote Point Sal, a nub of land north of Vandenberg Air Force Base and south of the Guadalupe Dunes. Windy Point Sal is a wall of bluffs rising 50 to 100 feet above the rocky shore. The water is crystal clear and the blufftops provide a fine spot to watch the boisterous seals and sea lions.

Point Sal was named by explorer Vancouver in 1792 for Hermenegildo Sal, at that time commandante of San Francisco. The state purchased the land in the 1940s. There are no facilities whatsoever at the beach, so remember, if you pack it in, pack it out.

This hike travels Point Sal State Beach, then takes to the bluffs above rocky reefs. At low tide you can pass around or over the reefs; at high tide the only passage is along the bluff trail. Both marine life and land life can be observed from the bluff trail. You'll pass a seal haul-out, tidepools, sight gulls, cormorant and pelicans, and perhaps see deer, bobcat and coyote on the ocean-facing slopes of the Casmalia Hills.

The trail system in the Point Sal area is in rough condition. The narrow bluff trails should not be undertaken by novice hikers, the weak-kneed or those afraid of heights. Families with small children and less experienced trekkers will enjoy beachcombing and tidepool-watching opportunities at Point Sal and the pleasure of discovering this out-of-the-way beach.

Directions to trailhead: From Highway 101 in Santa Maria, exit on Betteravia Road. Proceed west past a commercial strip and then out into the sugar beet fields. Betteravia Road twists north. About eight miles from Highway 101, turn left on Brown Road. Five miles of driving on Brown Road (watch for cows wandering along the road) brings you to a signed junction; leftward is a ranch road, but you bear right on Point Sal Road, partly paved, partly dirt washboard (impassable in wet weather). Follow this road 5 miles to its end at the parking area above Point Sal State Beach.

Be advised that Point Sal Road is sometimes closed during the rainy season. The Air Force sometimes closes the road for short periods during its missile launches.

For more information about Point Sal State Beach call the California Department of Parks and Recreation: (805) 733-3713.

The Walk: From the parking area, follow one of the short steep trails down to the beautiful crescent-shaped beach. Hike up-coast along the windswept beach. In 1/3 mile, you'll reach the end of the beach at a rocky reef, difficult to negotiate at high tide. A second reef, encountered shortly after the first, is equally difficult.

Unless it's very low tide, you'll want to begin following the narrow bluff trail above the reefs. The trail arcs westward with the coast, occasionally dipping down to rocky and romantic pocket beaches sequestered between reefs.

About 1 1/2 miles from the trailhead, you'll descend close to shore and begin boulder-hopping. After a few hundred yards of boulder-hopping, you'll begin to hear the bark of sea lions and get an aviator's view of Lion Rock, where the gregarious animals bask in the sun. Also be on the lookout for harbor seals, often called leopard seals because of their silver, white, or even yellow spots.

Your trek continues on a pretty decent bluff trail, which dips down near a sea lion haul-out. (Please don't approach or disturb these creatures.) You'll then ascend rocky Point Sal. From the point, you'll view the Guadalupe Dunes complex to the north and the sandy beaches of Vandenberg Air Force Base to the south. Before returning the same way, look for red-tailed hawks riding the updrafts and admire the ocean boiling up over the reefs.

Energetic hikers can follow a trail which passes behind Point Sal, joins a sandy road, and descends to a splendid beach north of the point. Here you'll find a two-mile long sandy beach to explore. This unnamed beach is almost always deserted except for a few fishermen and lots of pelicans.

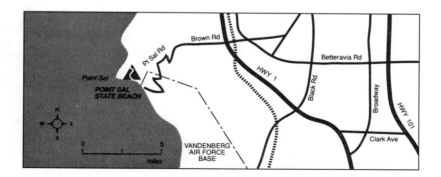

35
Nipomo Dunes Trail

Oso Flaco Lake to Coreopsis Hill: 2 1/2 miles round trip
Oso Flaco Lake to Santa Maria River: 8 miles round trip

The Nipomo Dunes are one of the largest relatively undisturbed dune complexes in California. The dunes, which run from the northern end of Pismo State Beach to Pt. Sal just north of Vandenburg Air Force Base, were in 1974 declared a national landmark by U.S. Secretary of the Interior Rogers Morton.

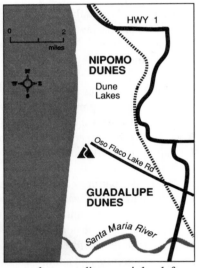

Three distinct dune fields—or "dune sheets" as they are sometimes called—make up the Nipomo Dunes: the Mussel Rock Dunes spread from the Santa Maria River south to Point Sal, the Guadalupe Dunes extend from Oso Flaco Lake south along the Santa Maria River drainage, and the Callender Dunes sprawl some distance inland from Arroyo Grande Creek south to Oso Flaco Lake.

The dunes are a dynamic ecosystem; they've been building up, shifting in response to the prevailing northwest winds, for the last 18,000 years or so. Some dunes continue to be formed today. The active, moving ones are those with little or no vegetation.

Flowers, plants and grasses are vital to the dune ecosystem because they stabilize the drifting sands. Brightening the dunes in the springtime are yellow and magenta sand verbena, coreopsis, daisies and white-fringed aster.

During the Great Depression, the dunes were home to the "Dunites," a motley collection of writers, artists, hermits, nudists and astrologers who lived in driftwood shacks and published their own magazine called "The Dune Forum." The dunes were featured in the 1964 movie, "The Great Race."

Shifting sands buried the Dunite community, as they had earlier buried more elaborate developments. In 1904, Oceano boasted beach cottages, a wharf, and mammoth La Grande Beach Pavillion. The developer's grandiose plans of turning Oceano into a tourist mecca did not materialize and the pavilion, wharf, and cottages were buried beneath advancing dunes.

This walk crosses the Nipomo Dunes and explores three more fascinating environments: Oso Flaco Lake, a 75-acre lake and marshland, Coreopsis Hill, where the giant "tree sunflower" thrives, and the mouth of the Santa Maria River.

Directions to trailhead: From Highway 1, three miles north of State Highway 166, turn west on Oso Flaco Road and drive 3 1/2 miles to road's end at the dunes.

The Walk: The wide path leads along Oso Flaco Creek, which is lined with goldenrod, watercress and rushes. In a quarter-mile the path reaches Oso Flaco, largest of the dune lakes. Actually, Oso Flaco Lakes, would be more accurate; both a "big" and "little" lake are situated here. Rails and grebes nest at water's edge, and sandpipers and a rather raucous duck population winter here.

The Portola Expedition camped at the lake in September, 1769. The soldiers killed a bear and feasted on it. Although Father Crespi, diarist and spiritual counselor for the expedition, wanted to call the lake "Lake of the Martyrs San Juan de Perucia and San Pedro de Sacro Terrato," the soldiers' more humble name of Oso Flaco or "lean bear" stuck.

From the lake, you'll walk oceanward along the creek, up and down the dunes to the water's edge and head south. Cross the creek, then cut eastward across the dunes.

Conspicuous by its dark green appearance, Coreopsis Hill stands out among its plainer, dun-colored neighboring dunes. February through April it's covered with Giant Coreopsis, sometimes reaching eight feet in height. A path leads up the western face of the dune.

From Coreopsis Hill, walk down the dunes to water's edge and head south. Three miles of beachwalking brings you to the Santa Maria River. Among the many native and migratory waterfowl residing in the wetland at the river mouth are the California least tern and the California brown pelican. Across the river is Rancho Guadalupe County Park, where you'll find the highest sand dune on the west coast, 450-foot tall Mussel Rock.

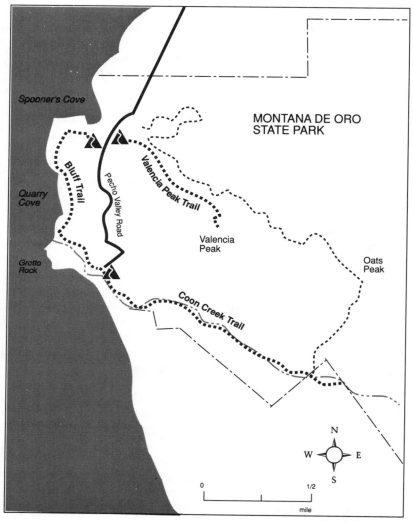

Spooner's Cove

MONTANA DE ORO
STATE PARK

Bluff Trail

Pecho Valley Road

Valencia Peak Trail

Quarry
Cove

Valencia
Peak

Oats
Peak

Grotto
Rock

Coon Creek Trail

N
W ⟡ E
S

0   1/2
mile

Trails 36, 37 38

36

Coon Creek Trail

Pecho Road to Old Shack: 5 miles round trip; 200-foot gain

Coon Creek is a year-round creek that winds through the Irish Hills along a lush canyon to the sea. The vegetation is so thick in the canyon that walkers often pass within a few feet of the creek, hear its murmuring, yet are unable to see it. Ancient Bishop pines line Coon Creek Canyon, which teems with wildlife—black-tailed deer, rabbits, possum, and, of course, raccoons.

This walk, one of the nicest in Montana de Oro State Park, follows the creek, crossing it a half-dozen times. Occasionally, the trail passes through meadowland seasonally blanketed with fiddleneck, poppies, mustard, and monkeyflowers. Beware: An extraordinary amount of poison oak grows along this trail.

Directions to the trailhead: From Highway 101, exit on Los Osos Road, continuing northwest for 12 miles until the road turns south to become Pecho Road. Pecho Road leads to Montana de Oro State Park. Continue four miles past the park entrance sign to road's end. A parking area is located at the trailhead.

The Walk: From the trailhead, you descend for a moment into a shallow canyon, then climb a ridge for a brief shoreline glimpse. The trail soon ventures into Coon Creek Canyon. You can hear but not see the creek on your right. The trail is choked with maple, willow, mugwort, and poison oak. A half-mile from the trailhead stand some Bishop pines.

Crossing and re-crossing the creek, the trail leads among live oaks covered with moss. At the two-mile mark, you ascend a short way into an exposed grassland that can either be considered a curse on hot days or a welcome repose from the poison oak. The meadow displays abundant wildflowers in spring. On your left, you'll spot the faint, unsigned Oats Peak Connector Trail. Trail's end occurs in a mixed stand of old oaks and cedars. Here you'll find the crumbling remains of an old shack.

On old topographic maps, Coon Creek Trail is shown extending for several more miles along the creek. Alas, you can continue but another tenth of a mile before hiking headlong into impenetrable thickets of poison oak.

Return the same way.

Bluffs Trail, Montana De Oro State Park

▲ 37
Montana De Oro Bluffs Trail

Spooner's Cove to Grotto Rock: 4 miles round trip

At the turn of the century, the greater portion of what is now known as Montana De Oro State Park was part of the Spooner Ranch. The most popular beach in the park is Spooner's Cove, whose isolation made it an ideal landing spot for contrabandistas during the Mission era, and for bootleggers during Prohibition.

This walk debarks from the south side of Spooner's Cove and travels atop rugged cliffs. Atop the bluffs grow fields of mustard and poppies, which give the park its "mountain of gold" name. Side trails drop to Spooner's and Coralina Coves, with fine tidepools to explore.

While hiking the bluffs, you may see harbor seals venturing ashore or otters diving for food beyond the surf line. Bird-watchers delight at the pelicans, albatross, cormorants and crimson-billed black oyster catchers.

Directions to the trailhead: See Walk #36 for directions to Montana de Oro State Park. The trail begins a hundred yards south of the campground, on the west side of Pecho Valley Road.

The Walk: The path crosses a dry creek on a footbridge and leads up to the bluffs overlooking Spooner's Cove.

A half-mile from the trailhead, a short fork to the right leads to Coralina Cove, bedecked with sea-polished broken shells and beautiful beach pebbles. The crystal-clear tidepools are full of anemones, starfish, mussels and colorful snails.

Continuing on the Bluffs Trail, you'll cross a wooden bridge. A mile from the trailhead is Quarry Cove, also with fine tidepools. The wide trail, lined with thistle and New Zealand spinach, eventually brings you to an overlook above some sea caves. Beyond is Grotto Rock.

You may return the same way, or bear left and return to the trailhead via Pecho Valley Road, or cross Pecho Valley Road to the trailhead for Coon Creek Trail. (See page 106 for map.)

Park trails offer grand views of the San Luis Obispo County coast

38

Valencia Peak Trail

Park Headquarters to Valencia Peak: 4 miles round trip; 1,300-foot gain

From a distance, you might suspect that 1,345-foot Valencia Peak is one of the morros-those distinct cone-shaped mountains that dot the San Luis Obispo County coast south of Morro Bay. However, Valencia Peak rose out of the sea in relatively recent geologic time. Geologists believed the processes that fashioned the mountain-tilting, folding, and upheaval occurred only five million years ago.

The peak's oceanic origins are revealed by its upper slopes, which were once beaches. You can find strands of beach sand and rocks that have been bored out by clams. Atop the mountain are fossil shells.

This walk switchbacks over what were once sea cliffs to the top of Valencia Peak, named after an Indian family, who lived nearby in the years after the Mission period. On fog-free days, the view of the central coast from Point Sal to Piedras Blancas is inspiring.

Directions to trailhead: See Walk #36 for directions to Montana de Oro State Park. Valencia Peak Trail begins at the signed trailhead across the campground road from park headquarters.

The Walk: The trail follows a (usually) mowed stretch of grass along Pecho Road to the south a few hundred yards, then turns inland and starts upslope to the east. Soon you'll be able to distinguish a series of marine terraces on the mountain. In spring, lupine, mustard, Indian paintbrush and a host of wildflowers cover the coastal slope.

A half-mile along, the trail bears left and heads directly toward the peak. You dip in and out of a dry gully and begin switchbacking over outcroppings of Monterey shale, traces of former sea cliffs.

As the trails levels out you'll go left at a trail junction, then begin switchbacking again, more steeply this time. The trail forks a bit below the peak: both trails go to the summit. Here you'll look out over the (mostly) unspoiled central coast. You can see the twenty-million-year-old volcanic peaks of Morro Rock, Hollister Peak, Black Mountain.

Look for fossils, enjoy the view, and return the same way. (See page 107 for a map of this trail.)

▲ 39
Morro Bay Sand Spit Trail

North end to Woodland Avenue: 4 miles one way

A walk along Morro Bay's sand-spit offers an opportunity to explore one of the Central coast's very special environments. The sand spit trail follows the sand dunes and ridges that separate Morro Bay on the inland side and Estero Bay on the ocean side. Atop some of the higher dunes (about 80 feet above sea level), you'll be treated to good vistas of the bay, Morro Rock, and nearby mountains.

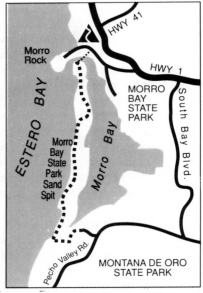

Heather, salt grass and coyote bush are among the hardy plants surviving in the harsh wind-lashed environment of the three-mile long sand spit. Silvery lupine, sea rocket and evening primrose add some seasonal color.

Bird-watchers may spot the snowy plover, which lays its eggs in the sand. On the muddy flats of the spit's bay side, willets, curlews and sandpipers feed.

Scientists say that a very high percentage of all sea life along the Central Coast originates in Morro Bay Estuary. Phenomenally nutritive waters of different salinities mix, creating an amazingly fecund environment. The triangular-shaped marsh, lined with eel grass and pickleweed, is an important spawning and nursery habitat for such fish as the California halibut and sand perch. Beneath the surface of the bay are oysters, clams, worms, snails, crabs and shrimp.

To learn more about the bay's ecology, animals and plant life, visit the Morro Bay Museum of Natural History, which is located in Morro Bay State Park. Exhibits are well done and the panoramic view of the bay is superb. For more information: (805) 772-2694.

A key element to this walk can be the Clam Taxi, a water-taxi service between the town of Morro Bay and the north end of the sand spit. Call (805) 772-8085 to be sure the taxi is running.

Directions to trailhead: Assuming the Clam Taxi is running, this walk begins in the town of Morro Bay at the marina at Pacific Street and Embarcadero.

Another way to reach the sand spit is to rent a canoe from the small marina located close to the Morro Bay Museum of Natural History. The shallow waters of the bay are a great place to practice your J-stroke.

If you want to arrange a car shuttle or begin the hike at the south end of the sand spit, here's how to reach the south trailhead: From Highway 101 in San Luis Obispo, exit on Los Osos Valley Road and head west through the town of Los Osos. One block after the road curves left to become Pecho Road, turn right on Woodland Avenue. Drive to the end of this road and park.

Clamming on the Morro Bay mudflats has long been a popular pastime

The Walk: From the end of the sand spit, where the Clam Taxi lands, walk south along the bay. The shoreline is silty, salty, and quite a contrast to the sandy dunes you'll be crossing farther south.

Dominating the seascape behind you is the "Gibraltar of the Pacific," 576-foot high Morro Rock, first sighted by Juan Cabrillo in 1542. The 50-million-year-old volcanic peak was used as a rock quarry from 1880 to 1969, but is now a wildlife preserve and part of the state park system. Atop Morro Rock roosts the endangered peregrine falcon, the quickest and most prized of falcons. The falcons are staging a comeback from the devastating effects of DDT, which caused them to lay thin fragile eggs.

A mile of bay-side walking brings you to Houseboat Cove.

Across the bay from the cove is Morro Bay Museum of Natural History. A heron rookery is in the cypress and eucalyptus grove near the museum. The herons nest in the treetops between February and June.

Continue another few hundred yards past the cove, then climb over the dunes to the ocean side of the sand spit. Walk south along surf's edge, which is littered with clam shells and sand dollars. After about 2 1/2 miles of travel, as the dunes on your left begin to recede, walk up a valley toward the top of the dunes.

You'll see a large shell mound in the center of the valley, a massive artifact left by the Chumash Indians. They piled clams, cockles, snails and even land game in these kitchen middens. (Inspect this shell mound and the others on the spit with care; they are protected archeological sites.) The bountiful marsh is so full of bird, land, and aquatic life that it's easy to imagine a large tribe of Chumash here; the men hunting rabbits in the dunes, the beautiful baskets of the women overflowing with shellfish.

From the top of the dunes, you'll get a good view of Morro Bay and spit's end at Shark's Inlet. Across the bay are the Morros, a series of extinct volcanoes that includes the famous Morro Rock. Rising behind the Morros are the Santa Lucia Mountains that stretch to Big Sur and beyond. This viewpoint is a good place to turn around and return to the trailhead at the north end of the spit.

If you have a car waiting at the south trailhead, descend the dunes to a dirt road, which you'll follow to a eucalyptus grove and trail's end at Woodland Avenue.

Hikers enjoy the high dunes of the Morro Bay State Park sand spit

▲ 40
Black Mountain Trail

Picnic Ground to Peak: 3 miles round trip; 600-foot gain

A series of nine peaks between San Luis Obispo and Morro Bay originated as volcanoes beneath the sea that covered this area 15 million years ago. After the sea and volcanic explosions subsided, erosion began dissolving the softer mountain material around the volcanic rock and left nine volcanic peaks standing high above the surrounding landscape. These volcanic plugs include Islay Peak in Montana De Oro State Park, Hollister Peak, and the famed Morro Rock.

Black Mountain, the last peak in the volcanic series before Morro Rock, has a trail that tours through a little of everything—chaparral, eucalyptus, oaks, pines, and coastal shrubs. From the mountain's 640-foot summit, you can see the Morro Bay Estuary, the sand spit, and the hills of nearby Montana De Oro State Park.

Directions to the trailhead: Follow Highway 1 twelve miles north of San Luis Obispo to the Los Osos-Baywood Park exit just before Morro Bay. Turn south on South Bay Boulevard and go 3/4 mile to Morro Bay State Park entrance. Bear left on the first fork beyond the entrance, heading 3/4 mile to the campground entrance. Park along the first crossroad inside the campground. Walk up the campground road to the picnic ground, where you'll see a pipe gate which indicates the beginning of the trail.

The Walk: Follow the Exercise Trail, cross a paved road and begin ascending more steeply. A mile from the trailhead, there's a junction. Bear left. The route becomes steeper, passing first through coastal shrubs, then conifers. The trail passes a water tank, then switchbacks to the summit.

After enjoying the fine view, you may return the same way or follow the following option.

Option: Return via East Fork of Exercise Trail: After you backtrack the 1/2 mile to the trail junction, go straight east. You'll discover a eucalyptus grove, where Monarch butterflies cluster. Cross a golf course road and rejoin the eastern section of the Exercise Trail, which returns you to the trailhead.

Morro Rock, "the Gibraltar of the Pacific," long a landmark to Coast travelers

41

Moonstone Beach Trail

Santa Rosa Creek to Leffingwell Landing: 2 1/2 miles round trip

Named for its moonstones (milky translucent agates), gravelly-shored Moonstone Beach is a great place for rockhounds. Moonstones and jaspers—types of quartz—were carried here by streams from the nearby coastal range and then polished by surf and sand.

From the bluffs above Moonstone Beach—part of San Simeon State Beach—the walker may observe sea otters; the beach marks the southern end of the California Sea Otter Game Refuge. During January and February, gray whale-watching is excellent here because the giants swim close to shore.

This walk begins at the mouth of Santa Rosa Creek, where there's a small freshwater lagoon. The path winds atop the bluffs above Moonstone Beach and visits Leffingwell Landing, the site of a pier once figuring prominently in the 19th-century coastal trade and now a fine picnic area.

Directions to trailhead: From Highway 1, just north of Cambria, turn west on Moonstone Beach Drive. Park at the Santa Rosa Creek day use area. (Moonstone Beach Drive intersects Coast Highway both north and south of Moonstone Beach.)

The Walk: Follow the bluff trail north from the parking area. The rugged headlands are undeveloped, in contrast to "Motel Row" on the east side of Moonstone Beach Drive. Moonstone Beach is composed of colored rocks.

A mile of walking brings you to the old highway bridge that spans Leffingwell Creek. Just above the creek is a state park day use area at Leffingwell Landing, where picnic tables are nestled in a sheltered cypress grove. During the 1870s and 1880s, ships unloaded lumber and other goods

118

here for the pioneer settlers who lived in the San Simeon Creek area.

The path picks up again at the bluff edge past the picnic area and winds through Monterey pine and cypress. Soon you'll be treated to views of Piedras Blancas Lighthouse to the north and Hearst Castle inland. Indian mortar holes are ground into the sandstone bluffs rising above the beach. You can either descend the bluffs to the beach or angle over to a vista point located near the point where Moonstone Beach Drive intersects Highway 1.

A rainy-day walk on Moonstone Beach

42

San Simeon Bay Trail

William Randolph Hearst State Beach to San Simeon Point:
2 miles round trip

A walk along San Simeon Bay is a nice diversion before or after a tour of "La Cuesta Encantada," the Enchanted Hill—name of the famous castle built by newspaper publisher William Randolph Hearst. The 146-room monument to the opulence of the Roaring '20s is one of the most popular tourist attractions in California.

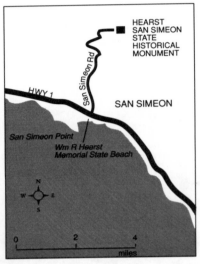

In the mid-1860s a severe drought wrecked the central coast cattle business and forced many debt-ridden Spanish rancheros to sell their land. Senator George Hearst bought out the rancheros and began developing his family estate. After the death of William Randolph Hearst in 1951, his heirs donated the beach south of Sebastian General Store for a park. It's a tranquil place; San Simeon Bay provides fairly good refuge from northwest and west winds. Fishing boats work the water nearby for albacore in summer and fall.

Directions to trailhead: William R. Hearst Memorial State Beach is located on San Simeon Road west of Highway 1. (Hearst San Simeon State Historical Monument is also located on San Simeon Road—east of the highway.) Park in the state beach day use lot or along San Simeon Road south of Sebastian General Store. The store was established in 1873 and is still in operation.

The Walk: Proceed through the picnic ground located in the eucalyptus grove just north of the fishing pier. When you reach the beach, turn up-coast. When the beach begins to arc westward, then ascend bluffs to a narrow dirt road leading atop the wooded bluff. This road, which narrows to a trail, offers fine coastline and castle views as it curves toward San Simeon Point. From the point are additional breathtaking views to the south of the

William Randolph Hearst's art collection is displayed throughout his castle

undeveloped San Luis Obispo County coast.

The path continues around the point on overgrown blufftop trails, then passes under the boughs of Monterey cypress on a dark tunnel-like trail for a quarter mile before re-emerging back on the bluffs. The bluff trails grow more faint and erratic as you descend a low sand dune to the beach. You can follow the beach until tides and rocks prevent further progress and you meet the Coast Highway quite some distance north.

▲ 43
Salmon Creek Trail

Coast Highway to Spruce Camp: 4 miles round trip; 800-foot gain
Coast Highway to Estrella Camp: 6 1/2 miles round trip; 1,200-foot gain
Coast Highway-Coast Ridge Rd., Return via Cruickshank-Buckeye Trails:
14 miles round trip; 3,000-foot gain

This walk, suitable for a strenuous day trip or more leisurely weekend backpack, offers a chance to sample the diversity of the coast range—lush fern canyons, fir forests, oak potreros—and sweeping views of the majestic coast and the Salinas Valley.

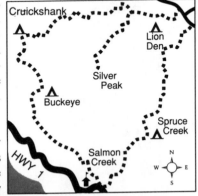

Directions to the trailhead: Salmon Creek Ranger Station (now closed, but it's a good landmark) is located a few miles north of the Monterey/San Luis Obispo County line off Highway 1. For those journeying from the north, the trailhead is some 75 miles south of Monterey. The trailhead is a hundred yards south of the station. Ample off-road parking is available at the station. The signed Salmon Creek Trail begins on the east side of the highway on the south side of the creek. At the beginning of the trail there's a great view of Salmon Creek Falls.

The Walk: Salmon Creek Trail immediately begins climbing, first through lush streamside vegetation, then across the exposed slopes of the canyon, covered with seasonal wildflowers. The lingering summer fog seems to protect the flowers here, and guards their display late into spring.

A thousand feet above sea level, the trail crosses a stream and ascends into a forest of Douglas fir, often called spruce—which helps explain the forthcoming destinations of Spruce Creek and Spruce Camp.

Two miles from the trailhead is the Spruce Creek Trail junction. The trail to the right leads south toward Dutra Spring and San Carpojo Creek. The main trail continues straight ahead up the main canyon of Salmon Creek. A few hundred yards of walking and you'll drop down to Spruce Creek Camp, located at the confluence of the waters of Salmon Creek and Spruce Creek. Spruce Creek Camp is in deep shade.

(If you're good at boulder-hopping and the creek isn't too high, it's possible to pick your way up Salmon Creek a mile to Estrella Camp. Remains of hydraulic mining equipment will be spotted en route.)

Our trail resumes on the other side of Spruce Creek and continues along the south slope of Salmon Creek. You cross a meadow where a cabin, believed to have been occupied by one of the hydraulic miners, once stood. The trail continues ascending moderately to Estrella Camp (1,500 feet), a grassy shady area along Salmon Creek. From here to Coast Ridge Road, there's no dependable source of water, so fill your canteen here. The trail soon rises above the last trees and ventures out onto the hot, brushy upper canyon slopes. You climb 1,800 feet in the next 2 1/2 miles, through an eroded area that is just recovering from a serious 1970 fire. This is a very hot stretch of trail in summer!

SALMON CREEK TRAIL
ESTRELLA CAMP 2½
SPRUCE CAMP 4
HIGHWAY 1 6

You reach the high point of the trail at Coast Ridge Road (3,120 feet), which marks the boundary between Fort Hunter Liggett Military Reservation and the National Forest. Bear left on the road. On clear days you'll be able to see the ocean to the west, the Salinas Valley to the east. In one-tenth mile, you'll reach the junction of the Cruickshank Trail. A sign indicates it's a mile to Lion's Den Camp, but it's more like one-half mile. A brief descent along a rough eroded road brings you to Lion's Den Camp, two small flat areas, often situated just above the coastal clouds. Water supply is from a small creek.

Leaving Lion's Den, you follow Silver Peak Road one-half mile to a junction. (Peak-baggers won't overlook Silver Peak (3,590 feet) on the left.) Cross the road and follow the Cruickshank Trail. The trail descends, crossing a creek, and drops a thousand feet in the next 2 1/2 miles. You'll get fine views of the Villa Creek drainage; in spring, waterfalls can be seen cascading down the canyon. Silver Camp, not shown on USFS maps, is a streamside camp with plenty of flat tenting sites.

Three-quarters of a mile from Silver Camp, you veer south on the Buckeye Trail. The path begins ascending through heavy timber, climbing the shady north slope. The trail descends to Redwood Creek, crossing it and proceeding in a southerly direction along the ridge separating Villa Creek and Redwood Creek Canyons. The trail grows more tentative as it enters a meadow and reaches Buckeye Camp, which has a developed spring.

Leaving the meadowland, you contour around to the western slopes, receiving the twin pleasures of ocean breezes and coastal views. You descend a ridge, cross Soda Springs Creek, and arrive at a signed junction. Buckeye Trail (now signed Soda Springs Trail) descends to Highway 1. This walk heads south, descending a mile through grassland and chaparral back to the trailhead.

⚠ 44

Vincente Flat Trail

Coast Highway to Espinosa Camp:
  6 1/2 miles round trip; 1,400-foot gain
Coast Highway to Vincente Flat Camp:
  10 miles round trip; 1,400-foot gain

Vincente Flat Trail provides an ideal introduction to the charms of Big Sur, for in five miles the walker experiences meadowland, coastal and canyon views, and a redwood forest. Vincente Flat is an ideal picnic site.

Directions to trailhead: Signed Vincente Flat Trailhead is located opposite Kirk Creek Campground on Highway 1, just north of the Nacimiento-Fergusson Road turnoff.

The Walk: The trail immediately begins ascending on a series of well-graded switchbacks through brush and grassland. Sweeping views of the coast from Jade Cove to Gamboa Point are yours. One nice feature of this walk is the way it alternates from sunny exposed slopes to shady redwood ravines. After topping a ridge, high point of Vincente Flat Trail, and enjoying fine coastal views, you'll enter the watershed of Hare Canyon.

Tiny Espinosa Camp (1,780 feet) is 3 1/4 miles from the trailhead. Water is 1/4 mile up-trail, where a tiny unnamed creek cascades down a redwood-lined ravine to the trail.

The trail ascends briefly, then makes a short descent to Hare Creek and follows it. After crossing the creek, the walker encounters signed Stone Ridge Trail Junction located on a low rise above the creek. To reach Vincente Flat Campground, take the Girard Trail to the right upstream 150 yards. Redwoods shade idyllic campsites. Water usually flows, even in summer, and a lovely meadow beckons picnickers and sun worshipers.

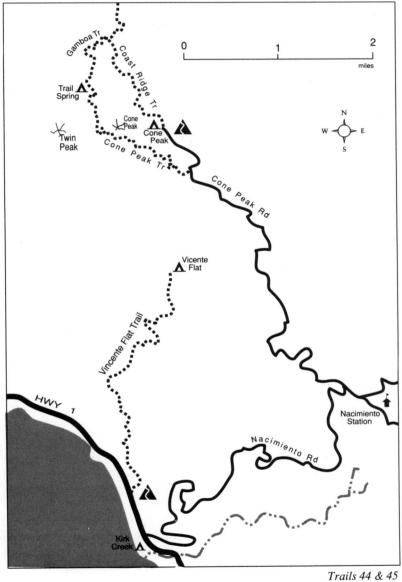

Trails 44 & 45

45

Cone Peak Trail

Coast Ridge Road to Cone Peak: 4 miles round trip; 1,200-foot gain

Cone Peak, a geographical landmark to coast travelers for more than a hundred years, is the most abrupt pitch of country along the Pacific Coast. It rises to 5,155 feet in about 3 1/2 miles from sea level. On a clear day in winter, as you stand on Sand Dollar Beach, the snow-covered peak is a stirring sight.

Botanically, Cone Peak is a very important mountain. On its steep slopes botanists Thomas Coulter and David Douglas discovered the Santa Lucia fir, considered the rarest and most unique fir in North America. (Tree lovers know that when names were attached to western cone-bearing trees, Coulter's went to a pine, Douglas' to a fir.) The spire-like Santa Lucia fir, or Bristlecone fir, is found only in scattered stands in northern San Luis Obispo and southern Monterey counties in the Santa Lucia Mountains. Typically, this fir occurs above the highest coast redwoods (about 2,000 feet) within mixed evergreen forest. Santa Lucia fir concentrates in steep, rocky, fire-resistant spots at elevations from 2,000 to 5,000 feet.

Directions to the trailhead: From Highway 1, four miles south of Lucia and just south of Kirk Creek Campground, or about 9 miles north of Gorda, turn east on Nacimiento-Fergusson Road. This road provides dramatic coastal views as it ascends sharply 7 miles to Nacimiento Summit. At the signed junction at the summit, turn left on graded Coast Ridge Road (Cone Peak Road) and follow it 5 miles north along the ridge to the signed trail junction on the west side of the road. Parking is adequate for a few cars. (Warning: During the rainy season, Cone Peak Road may be sometimes closed.)

The Walk: The well-graded trail ascends through tan oak woodland. Soon the trail begins a series of steep switchbacks through brush. You'll enjoy views of Santa Lucia fir and Coulter pine. As the trail gains elevation, sugar pine predominates.

Hikers reach a signed junction 1 3/4 miles from the trailhead. (A trail leads west 1 1/4 miles down to steep, deeply shaded Trail Springs Camp (3,800 feet). For an interesting loop around Cone Peak, you can pick up the Gamboa Trail and ascend another 1 1/4 miles to the Coast Ridge Trail. You can then follow Coast Ridge Trail to its junction with Coast Ridge Road and follow the road a mile back to your car.)

From this junction, the main trail ascends a final 1/4 mile eastward to the fire lookout atop Cone Peak summit. The lookout is staffed during fire season. Fine views of the valleys to the east and coastline to the west are yours. Spreading before you is a panorama of peaks: Pinyon Peak, Ventana Double Cone, Junipero Serra Peak, Uncle Sam Mountain.

Return the same way, or hike the optional loop through Trail Springs Camp and around the great peak. (See page 127 for map.)

Cone Peak Trail, 1920

46

Waterfall Trail

McWay Canyon to McWay Falls: 3/4 mile round trip

A redwood grove, dramatic coastal vistas, and the only major California waterfall to tumble into the Pacific are some of the attractions awaiting the walker at Julia Pfeiffer Burns State Park. An easy "leg stretcher" walk leads to an overlook above the dramatic and much-photographed McWay Falls.

The park is a tribute to hardy pioneer Julia Pfeiffer Burns, remembered for her deep love of the Big Sur backcountry. Her father, Michael Pfeiffer, started a ranch in the Santa Lucia Mountains in 1869. In 1915, Julia Pfeiffer married John Burns, and the two ran a cattle ranch while living at their ranch in McWay Canyon.

During the 1920s, New York congressman and confidante to President Franklin Roosevelt, Lathrop Brown, and his wife Helen, built "Waterfall House" on the bluffs above McWay Falls. Built before the completion of Coast Highway, the isolated residence was surrounded by a lush garden of plants imported from around the world. Easterner Helen Brown was an admirer of westerner Julia Pfeiffer Burns, and in 1962, more than three decades after her friend's death, she donated the Brown's property to the state. Helen Brown also requested that Waterfall House become a park museum; however, the parks department insisted that it lacked sufficient funds to operate a museum and bulldozed the house into the sea.

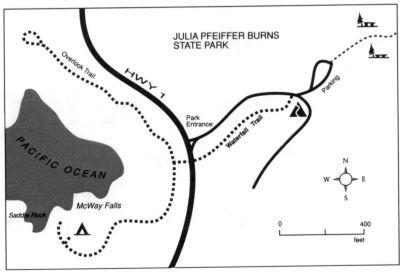

*McWay Falls,
Julia Pfeiffer Burns
State Park*

Directions to trailhead: Julia Pfeiffer Burns State Park is located about 36 miles south of Carmel and some 10 miles south of Pfeiffer Big Sur State Park. Turn east into the park and proceed to the day use lot.

The Walk: Take the signed trail toward Scenic Overlook. Along McWay Creek you'll spot some eucalyptus, quite a botanical contrast to the redwoods growing up creek. Ceanothus and dogwood splash spring color along the trail. The path leads through a tunnel under Coast Highway and emerges to offer the walker grand panoramas of the Big Sur coast. You'll soon reach the overlook, where you can observe the slender, but dramatic waterfall tumbling a hundred feet from the granite cliffs into McWay Cove.

On your return, you can take a side trail and meander over to the park's cypress-shaded environmental campsites, which are perched on the former site of Waterfall House. When you arrive back at the trailhead, consider following the park trail to the picnic area located in a lovely redwood grove.

131

47

Partington Cove Trail

1/2 mile round trip: 200-foot loss

Partington Cove, part of Julia Pfeiffer Burns State Park, was once the site of a dock where tanbark was loaded onto waiting ships. Woodsmen stripped the tanbark oak, a kind of cross between an oak and a chestnut. Before synthetic chemicals were invented to tan leather, gathering and shipping of the bark was a considerable industry along the Big Sur coast. During the 1880s, homesteader John Partington operated a landing here.

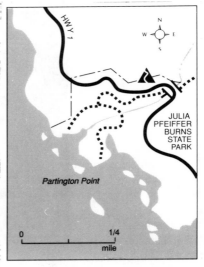

This short leg-stretcher of a walk drops down to Partington Creek and over to the deep blue waters of the cove.

Directions to trailhead: Partington Cove Trail begins 1.8 miles north of Julia Pfeiffer Burns State Park entrance at the point where Highway 1 crosses Partington Creek.

The Walk: From an iron gate, follow the dirt road that drops down into the canyon cut by Partington Creek. (A steep side trail continues down to the tiniest of beaches at the creek mouth.) The main trail crosses the creek on a wooden footbridge and passes through a hundred-foot-long tunnel that was blasted through the rocky cliffs.

At Partington Cove are the remains of a dock. The not-so-placid waters of the cove stir the seaweed about as if in a soup, and you wonder how boats moored here actually manged to load their cargo of bark and lumber.

Offshore, between Partington Point and McWay Creek to the south, is Julia Pfeiffer Burns Underwater Area, placed under state protection in 1970. Kelp forests provide habitat for abalone, lingcod and many more sea creatures, as well as for otters, which you may glimpse if you follow the crumbling cliffside trail from the dock site to the end of Partington Point.

▲ 48
Pine Ridge Trail

Big Sur Station to Ventana Camp Junction:
4 1/4 miles one way; 1,100-foot gain
Big Sur Station to Barlow Flat:
7 miles one way; 1,100-foot gain
Big Sur Station to Sykes Camp:
10 miles one way; 1,100-foot gain
Big Sur Station to Redwood Camp:
12 miles one way; 1,400-foot gain

Sykes Camp on the east bank of the Big Sur River has a little bit of everything—morning sun, afternoon shade, a deep swimming hole and a hot spring. Only ten miles from Pfeiffer Big Sur State Park, Sykes Camp is a (too) popular destination. Most visitors are of the mellow variety, but others lack wilderness manners and leave litter behind. Drinking water taken from the river should most certainly be purified.

Sykes' charms are undeniable, but seekers of solitude should steer clear in the summer months. Rangers report that nearly 80 percent of the backcountry use taking place in the Monterey District of Los Padres National Forest occurs along the ten miles from the state park to Sykes.

Directions to trailhead: Pine Ridge Trail begins at Big Sur Ranger Station, located east of Highway 1 just south of the entrance to Pfeiffer Big Sur State Park. A kiosk at the entrance to the parking lot sells maps and dispenses wilderness permits (necessary for this walk).

The Walk: From the edge of the parking area, Pine Ridge Trail ascends rapidly, soon leaving behind the redwoods and Big Sur River Valley. Mount Manuel dominates the northern skyline, while glimpses of the Pacific can be seen behind you.

The trail climbs through chaparral and woodland on its eastern ascent. After a little over 4 miles of climbing, the trail reaches a junction with a side trail leading to Ventana Camp, located 1 1/4 mile north. (For a walk of a little over 10 miles round trip, take the trail to the camp, located near the convergence of Ventana Creek and the Big Sur River. In 1968, the camp achieved notoriety when the U.S. Forest Service closed it for a time due to "the hippie problem." Near the camp is a great swimming hole. After lunch and a swim, return to Big Sur Station.)

Pine Ridge Trail

Pine Ridge Trail continues east a mile to another side trail; this one leads a short distance to redwood-shaded Terrace Creek Camp. This destination, too, would be an ideal lunch stop/turnaround point for a day hike.

Pine Ridge Trail crosses Terrace Creek, ascends through woodland, descends a hill and crosses Logwood Creek, and arrives at Barlow Flat. This flat expansive camp is situated on the north side of the Big Sur River in the shade of redwoods. It's especially popular with fishermen.

Leaving Barlow Flat, the trail stays above the river for another three miles until it reaches Sykes Camp. The hot spring is 1/4 mile downriver and flows south of the riverbank. You'll enjoy basking in the 100-degree mineral waters, gazing up at the stars in the night sky.

Two more miles of travel on the Pine Ridge Trail will bring you to Redwood Creek Camp, which has several stoves and tent sites. It's a rarely visited alternative to Sykes Camp.

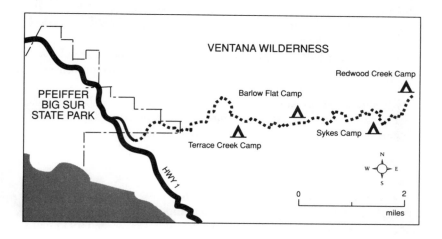

49

Pfeiffer Beach Trail

Sycamore Canyon Road to Pfeiffer Beach: 3/4 mile round trip

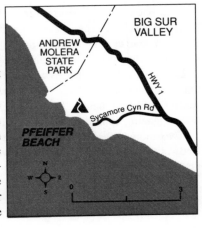

Los Padres is one of only three national forests in America with ocean frontage. Named for the pioneer Pfeiffer family, this secluded white sand beach faces the turbulent sea which sends awesome waves crashing through blowholes in the rocks. Many scenes from the film "The Sandpipers," with Elizabeth Taylor and Richard Burton, were shot here. The magic of motion pictures gave us a calm beach where small boats easily landed. Big Sur residents laugh every time this movie is shown on late-night TV.

With its hazardous surf and gusty winds, Pfeiffer Beach cannot be said to be a comfortable stretch of coastline; it is however, a magnificent one.

Directions to the trailhead: Driving south, a mile south of Big Sur State Park entrance, take the second right-hand turn off Highway 1 (west). Sycamore Canyon Road is a sharp downhill turn. Follow the two-mile narrow, winding and sometimes washed-out road to the Forest Service parking area.

The Walk: Follow the wide sandy path leading from the parking lot through the cypress trees. Sycamore Creek empties into a small lagoon near the beach. Marvel at the sea stacks, blowholes and caves, and try to find a place out of the wind to eat your lunch. The more ambitious may pick their way over rocks northward for a mile around a point to a second crescent-shaped beach.

Early Forest Rangers enjoy the Big Sur coastline; Pfeiffer Beach is one of several national forest coastal locales

The Pfeiffer family's rustic resort welcomed forest visitors

 **50**

Valley View Trail

Big Sur Lodge to Pfeiffer Falls, Valley View:
2 miles round trip; 200-foot gain

For most visitors, 'Big Sur' means Pfeiffer Big Sur State Park. The state park-and its brief but popular trail system-is dominated by the Big Sur River, which meanders through redwood groves on its way to the Pacific Ocean, five miles away.

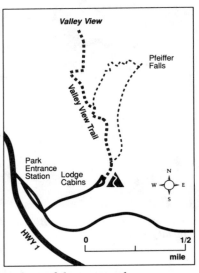

John Pfeiffer, for whom the park was named, homesteaded 160 acres of mountainous terrain between Sycamore Canyon and the Big Sur River. In 1884 he moved into a cabin perched above the Big Sur River Gorge. (You can see the reconstructed "Homestead Cabin," which is located on the park's Gorge Trail.) John Pfeiffer sold and donated some of his ranchland to the state in the 1930s, and it became the nucleus of the state park.

This walk, which follows the Pfeiffer Falls Trail and Valley View Trail, is an easy "leg stretcher" suitable for the whole family. It visits Pfeiffer Falls and offers a good introduction to the delights of the state park.

Directions to trailhead: Pfeiffer Big Sur State Park is located off Highway 1, some 26 miles south of Carmel and 2 miles south of the hamlet of Big Sur. There is a state park day use fee, payable at the park entry kiosk. Beyond the entry booth, turn left at the stop sign, then veer right toward the cottages of Big Sur Lodge. Very soon, you'll find some day use parking. A much larger parking area is located near the store and restaurant.

The Walk: From the signed trailhead, follow the trail to Pfeiffer Falls. Very shortly, on your left, you'll spot a trail heading left to Valley View; this will be your return path. The walk continues under stately redwoods and meanders along with Pfeiffer-Redwood Creek.

You'll soon ascend a redwood stairway to a junction with Oak Grove Trail, which leads rightward 1 1/2 miles through oak and madrone woodland

Big Sur River

over to the Mt. Manuel Trail. Stay left at this junction and follow Pfeiffer Falls Trail through the forest and past a second branch of the Valley View Trail. A stairway leads to an observation platform at the base of the falls. Pfeiffer-Redwood Creek cascades over a 40-foot precipice to a small grotto.

After enjoying the falls, descend the stairway and bear right on the Valley View Trail, which leaves behind the redwoods and ascends into a tanbark oak and coast live oak woodland.

At a signed junction, turn right and follow the pathway along a minor ridge to a lookout. The Pacific Ocean pounding the Point Sur headlands and the Big Sur River Valley are part of the fine view.

Backtrack along Valley View Trail and at the first junction stay right and descend back to Pfeiffer-Redwood Canyon. Another right at the canyon bottom brings you back to the trailhead.

▲ 51
River Trail

Highway 1 to Molera Point: 2 1/2 miles round trip

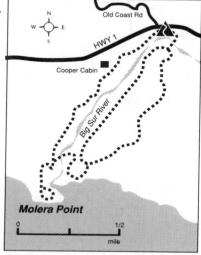

Mountains, meadows and the mouth of Big Sur River are some of the highlights of a walk through Andrew Molera State Park.

Yankee fur trader Juan Bautista Roger Cooper acquired this land, formerly part of the Mexican land grant Rancho El Sur, in 1855. Acquaintances of his day—and historians of today—speculate that Cooper used his "Ranch of the South" as a landing spot, bringing cargo ashore at the Big Sur River mouth in order to avoid the high custom fees of Monterey Harbor.

Grandson Andrew Molera, who inherited the ranch, had a successful dairy operation; his Monterey Jack cheese was particularly prized. He was a hospitable fellow, popular with his neighbors who camped along the river while awaiting shipments of supplies from San Francisco.

Beach Trail follows the north bank of the Big Sur river to the ocean and River Trail meaders with the river's south bank back to the trailhead. A diversity of river ecosystems, including redwoods and a eucalyptus grove where monarch butterflies overwinter, await the walker.

Directions to trailhead: Andrew Molera State Park is located off Highway 1, 21 miles south of Carmel.

The Walk: From the parking area, follow the trail to the campground. The path parallels the river, which is crowded with thimbleberry and blackberry, honeysuckle vines, willow and bay laurel. At the river mouth is a small beach and a shallow lagoon, frequented by sanderlings, willets and many more shorebirds. A short trail leads above the beach to Molera Point.

Pick up the trail to the right (south) side of the river. It ascends through coastal scrub, then dips with the rolling grasslands of Creamery Meadows.

The trail continues along the river and over a bridge back to the trailhead.

52

Pt. Sur Lightstation Trail

1/2 mile guided walk: 250-foot gain

During the nineteenth century, when coastal roads were few and poor, most cargo was transported by ship. Ships traveled close to shore so that when storms occurred they could take advantage of protection offered by bay and point. This heavy coastal trade—and its dangers—prompted the U.S. Lighthouse Service Board to establish a series of lighthouses along California's coast located about sixty miles apart.

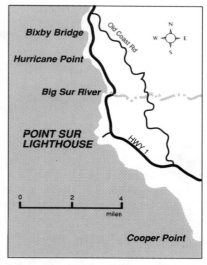

Point Sur had been the death of many ships, and mariners had been petitioning for a beacon for many years when the government in 1885 appropriated $50,000 to construct a lightstation. The Point Sur light joined the one at Piedras Blancas situated 60 miles south and the one located 60 miles north at Pigeon Point.

The first light, which became operational in 1889, utilized one of the famed Fresnel lenses, designed by the French physicist Augustin Jean Fresnel. A whale oil lantern was the first light source. In later years, kerosene fueled the operation.   Soot problems from the not-very-clean burning kerosene kept the keepers busy polishing the glass and worrying about surprise visits from supervisors who conducted "white glove" inspections.

The lighthouse became fully automated in 1975. The original light, visible for 23 miles out to sea, is now on display in the Allen J. Knight Maritime Museum in Monterey.

The century-old stone buildings, when viewed from Highway 1, are intriguing; they're even more fascinating when viewed up close on one of the tours conducted by the Point Sur Lightstation Docents Association. While the station undergoes restoration, the only way to see the facility—the only intact lightstation with accompanying support buildings on the California coast—is by guided tour.

Pt. Sur Lightstation

The tour includes the lighthouse itself, the keepers' houses, the blacksmith shop and the barn, where livestock was kept for food and transportation. You'll learn the fascinating story of the isolated life lived by the four keepers and their families.

The walk to the lighthouse is interesting for more than historical reasons. Geology buffs will call the path to the light the "Tombolo Trail"; a tombolo, rare on the California coast, is a sand bar connecting an island to the mainland.

The view from atop the 270-foot high basaltic rock is superb. You're eyeball-to-eyeball with the gulls and cormorants. To the south is False Sur, named for its confusing resemblance to Point Sur when viewed from sea.

In 1980, Point Sur Lightstation was designated a state historic landmark, and in 1984 the U.S. Department of the Interior turned it over to the California Department of Parks and Recreation. The old Lighthouse Service Board was long ago absorbed by the U.S. Coast Guard, and the kerosene lamp and steam-driven warning whistle have been replaced by a computer-directed electric beam and radio beacon, but Point Sur Lightstation, as it has for a century, continues to warn ships of the treacherous Big Sur Coast.

Docent-led tours are currently offered on Sundays, at 10:00 a.m. and 1:00 p.m.. For more details about Point Sur State Historic Park and lightstation tours, contact the State Department of Parks and Recreation at Pfeiffer Big Sur State Park: (408) 667-2316.

53

Rocky Ridge Trail

Return via Soberanes Canyon Trail: 7 miles round trip; 1,200-foot gain

Undeveloped, and usually overlooked, Garrapata State Park offers a lot of Big Sur in a compact area. Rocky Ridge Trail quickly leaves Highway 1 behind and offers far-reaching views of the Santa Lucia Mountains and the sea. A grand loop trip can be made by returning to the trailhead via redwood-lined Soberanes Canyon.

The name Soberanes is linked with the early Spanish exploration of California. Soldier Jose Maria Soberanes marched up the coast to Monterey with the Gaspar de Portola expedition of 1769. Seven years later, Soberanes served as a guide for De Anza, whose party pushed north to San Francisco Bay. Grandson Jose Antonio Ezequiel Soberanes acquired the coastal bluff and magnificent backcountry that became known as Soberanes Ranch.

Bear hunter/buckskin trader/butcher/steam ship agent William Brainard Post was an early foreman of Soberanes Ranch. His son, Joseph William Post, was born on the ranch. In 1888, the younger Post was awarded the government contract to build a road to the top of Point Sur Lightstation.

Directions to trailhead: Garrapata State Park is located on Highway 1, about 4 miles south of Point Lobos State Reserve. Some parking is available on the inland side of the highway near the old barn, where the trail begins. More parking is available on the highway shoulder.

The Walk: The trail begins behind the old barn. It crosses Soberanes Creek and almost immediately forks. Go leftward on the Rocky Ridge Trail, which for a short distance follows an old ranch road. Soon you veer inland on a steep trail.

You rapidly leave the highway behind as the path climbs the rugged slopes, which are dotted with black sage, golden yarrow and bush lupine. The route uses few switchbacks as it ascends 1,435-foot high Rocky Ridge. As you gain the wind-blown ridge, you'll get a good views to the east of Soberanes Creek watershed, to the west of Soberanes Point, and to the north of Carmel.

The route contours eastward around the ridge. To the north, is the steep canyon cut by Malpaso Creek. After leveling out for a time, the grassy path reaches a small cow pond, then begins to descend over steep, but pastoral, terrain—classic Big Sur cattle country.

In spring, the emerald-green slopes resemble Ireland. The grassland on

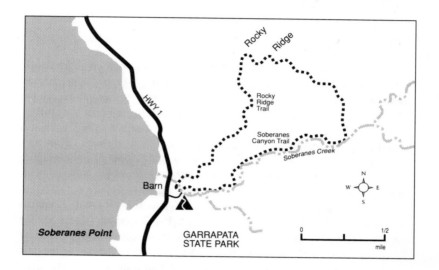

Rocky Ridge

Rocky Ridge Trail

Soberanes Canyon Trail

Soberanes Creek

HWY 1

Barn

Soberanes Point

GARRAPATA STATE PARK

N
W — E
S

0   1/2
mile

these upper slopes is extensive. The hillsides would naturally be covered with coastal scrub vegetation, but introduced grasses—wild oats, ryegrass, and foxtail—have taken over.

The trail is cut by cattle paths, a reminder of a century of grazing. Your route plunges very steeply down the bald, north wall of Soberanes Canyon. In the shade of the canyon, you intersect Soberanes Canyon Trail and descend to the west.

Soberanes Canyon Trail stays close to the creek, and enters the redwoods. The canyon redwoods are smaller and fewer than those found to the north. Soberanes Canyon is near the southern end of their range. Western sword fern, redwood sorrel, blackberry bushes and Douglas iris decorate the path.

As you near the mouth of the canyon, the trail gentles. Willow, watercress, and horsetail line the lower reaches of Soberanes Creek. The old barn, where you began this walk, is also trail's end.

54

Cypress Grove Trail

3/4-mile round trip

Sometimes it's the tranquil moments at Point Lobos you remember: Black-tailed deer moving through the forest, the fog-wrapped cypress trees. And sometimes it's nature's more boisterous moments that you recall: the bark of sea lions at Sea Lion Point, the sea thundering against the cliffs.

A visit to Point Lobos State Reserve, in good weather or bad, is always memorable. Landscape artist Francis McComas called Point Lobos "the greatest meeting of land and water in the world." Some of photographer Ansel Adams' greatest work was inspired by the wind-sculpted cypress, lonely sentinels perched at the edge of the continent.

Here at Point Lobos, the Monterey cypress makes a last stand. Botanists believe that during Pleistocene times, some half-million years ago, when the climate was wetter and cooler than it is now, huge forests of cypress grew along the coast—indeed, throughout North America. When the world's climate warmed, the cypress retreated to a few damp spots. Nowadays, the grove at Point Lobos and another across Carmel Bay at Cypress Point are the only two native stands in existence.

The Monterey cypress, with the help of humans, can cross hot and dry regions and become established in cool areas elsewhere. In fact, this rare conifer is easily grown from seed and has been successfully distributed all over the world, so it's puzzling why the tree's natural range is so restricted.

Cypress Grove Trail visits Allan Memorial Grove, which honors A. M.

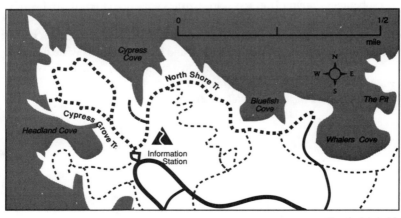

Trails 54 & 55

Allan who, in the early years of this century, helped preserve Point Lobos from resort developers. Allan, a farmer and dairyman, lived across the Coast Highway from what is now the reserve. Developers were dividing "Point Lobos City" into tiny 25-foot lots, when Allan began his conservation efforts. In an attempt to keep the Point intact, he bought some of the lots. In later years, when autos and picnickers came in great numbers, Allan set up a toll gate. When Point Lobos became a reserve in 1933, Allan's family gave the cypress grove to the state.

Cypress Grove Trail wanders through the cypress and offers great tree-framed views of Carmel Bay and Monterey peninsula.

Directions to trailhead: Point Lobos State Reserve is located three miles south of Carmel just off Highway 1. There is a state park day use fee. The trail departs from the northwest end of the Cypress Grove parking area.

The reserve has an excellent interpretive program. Docent-led walks explore the trails and tidepools.

The Walk: A short distance from the information station at the trailhead, the path splits. The right fork is the beginning of the North Shore Trail. Bear left. Before reaching the cypress grove, the path cuts through a chaparral environment. During early spring, the ceanothus (wild lilac) blossoms pink and blue.

Behind you are the rocky islands off Sea Lion Point. The Spaniards called the domain of these creatures "Punto de los Lobos Marinos"—Point of the Sea Wolves. You'll probably hear the barking of the sea lions before you see them.

A short side trail leads to North Point and a good view of Big Dome and Cypress Cove. Another side trail offers a vista of Monterey peninsula and Carmel Bay.

The main path winds through the cypress grove. Coastward is The Pinnacle, northernmost point in the reserve. Winds off the Pacific really batter this point and the exposed trees. To combat the wind, the trees adopt a survival response called buttressing: a narrow part of the trunk faces the wind while the trunk grows thicker on the other side in order to brace itself. The wind-sculpted trunks and wind-shaped foliage give the cypress their fantastic shapes.

The path turns south past South Point and returns to the trailhead.

▲ 55
North Shore Trail

Sea Lion Point Parking to Whalers Cove: 3 miles round trip

Less celebrated than the Monterey cypress but almost as rare, the Monterey pine is found growing naturally within Point Lobos State Reserve and at only two other areas along the California coast. This fog-loving, three-needled pine has a very restricted natural range; however, it's cultivated for timber all over the world—particularly in the South Pacific.

North Shore Trail wanders through the pines and offers terrific coastal panoramas. Watchers of the late, late show and admirers of spooky beauty will enjoy the shrouds of pale green lichen hanging from the dead branches of the Monterey pines. Lichen, which conducts the business of life as a limited partnership of algae and fungae, is not a parasite and does not hurt the tree. It's believed that the presence of lichen is an indication of extremely good air quality.

The coastal trails of Point Lobos—the North Shore Trail among them—are fine places to watch for gray whales on their annual migration. The best times to see the giants are January, when they swim south, and the end of March, when they swim north.

Whalers Cove, visited by North Shore Trail, is the site of an 1861-1884 whaling operation. Portuguese whalers hauled the harpooned whales into the cove, butchered their catch in the water, and boiled the blubber into oil on shore.

North Shore Trail offers bird's-eye views of Guillemot Island and a number of dramatic coves.

Directions to trailhead: See Walk #55 for directions to Cypress Grove Trail.

The Walk: The trail leading north from the information station soon splits. Take the right fork. Soon you'll pass the short Old Veteran Trail that offers a view of the lonely Old Veteran Cypress perched on the rocks above Cypress Cove.

North Shore Trail heads through the cypress in East Grove and gives you a view of Guillemot Island. A variety of birds nest atop this large offshore rock and others. Pigeon guillemots, cormorants and gulls are some of the birds you might see.

Point Lobos

Offshore is the Point Lobos Underwater Reserve, America's first such reserve, set aside in 1960. Divers explore the 100-foot high kelp forests in Whalers and Blue Fish Cove. Mineral rich waters from the nearby 1,000-foot deep Carmel Submarine Canyon upwell to join the more shallow waters of the coves.

At Whalers Cove, where divers enter the underwater reserve, you'll find some interpretive displays about underwater life.

After Portuguese whalers left California, Japanese fishermen gathered abalone from Whalers Cove. A cannery situated on the north end of Whalers Cove—Cannery Point—hundreds of thousands of abalone were canned and shipped to Asia.

You may retrace your steps to the trailhead or return via Whalers Knoll Trail. Watch for deer and rabbits browsing along this path. The trail ascends to a hilltop, where a whale-watching lookout once stood. You'll intersect North Shore Trail a quarter-mile from the trailhead. (See page 146 for map of trail.)

56

Carmel River State Beach

River mouth to Monastery Beach: 2 miles round trip

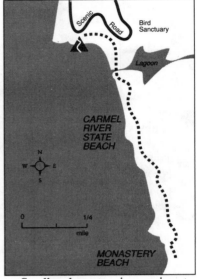

Carmel River, which arises high on the eastern slopes of the Santa Lucia Mountains and empties into the sea just south of Carmel, is a river of many moods. Some of its forks, swollen by winter and spring rains, can be capricious, frothy waterways as they course through the Ventana Wilderness. Tamed by Los Padres Dam on the northern boundary of the national forest, the river's descent through Carmel Valley is relatively peaceful.

At its mouth, too, the Carmel River has differing moods and appearances. About May a sandbar forms, turning the river mouth into a tranquil lagoon. During winter, the river bursts through the berm and rushes to the sea. Steelhead trout swim up river to spawn.

At the north end of Carmel River State Beach is a brackish lagoon, where shorebirds feed. Carmel River Bird Sanctuary is here and even the most casual bird-watcher will be impressed by the abundance of waterfowl. Ducks, mallards and coots patrol the lagoon. Egrets and herons stand amongst the reeds. Hawks hover overhead. Bring your binoculars.

This walk explores the river mouth, then travels the length of Carmel River State Beach to a point just north of Point Lobos named Monastery Beach, for the Carmelite Monastery located just across Highway 1 from the shore.

Directions to trailhead: During the summer and autumn months, the sandy berm at the Carmel River mouth provides a fine path between river and sea. At this time of year, you can start this walk at the north end of Carmel State Beach. From Highway 1, just south of the town of Carmel, turn west on Rio Road. When you reach Santa Lucia Street, turn left, then proceed 5 more blocks to Carmel Street. Turn left and follow this road to the beach.

You can also start at the south end of Carmel River State Beach, easily accessible from Highway 1.

The Walk: Follow the shoreline down coast over the sandy berm. In places, the route is rocky, the domain of nervous crabs, who scatter at your approach. You'll surely notice the iceplant-lined path above the beach; save this path for the return trip.

After rounding a minor point and passing some wind-bent Monterey cypress, you'll arrive at Monastery Beach—also known as San Jose Creek Beach, for the creek that empties onto the northern end of the beach. With the chimes from the nearby monastery ringing in your ears, you might be lulled into thinking that Monastery Beach is a tranquil place, but it's not; the surf is rough and the beach drops sharply off into the sea. Even the most experienced swimmers should be ultracautious.

For a little bit different return route, take the state beach service road, which farther north becomes a trail. This dirt road/trail, just before reaching the lagoon, climbs a small hill where a large cross is implanted. The cross was erected by the Carmel Mission in 1944, and is similar to the one put here by the 1769 Portola expedition in order to signal the Spanish ship that was to resupply them. Unfortunately, the expedition did not realized how close it was to its intended destination—Monterey Bay—and turned back south.

From the cross, follow a path down slope and intersect another path that leads along the south bank of the Carmel River. Follow the berm and beach back to the trailhead.

57

Monterey Bay Trail

Fisherman's Wharf to Monterey Bay Aquarium: 2 miles round trip

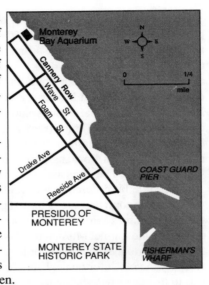

Before the 1849 gold rush and overnight rise of the city and port of San Francisco, Monterey was the political and commercial center of California. A waterfront walk of Monterey offers a glimpse backwards at this time—and to other colorful periods of the city's history.

Monterey is probably most identified with its world-renowned sardine canning industry, but the city has hosted many other enterprises that reflect the diverse ethnic heritage of California. Monterey's storied shores have been the work site for Mexican customs officials, Yankee traders, Portuguese whalers, as well as Chinese and Italian fishermen.

As a supplement to this walk, which stays close to the waterfront, be sure to venture downtown along the self-guided "Monterey Path of History." This tour visits many of the buildings within Monterey State Historic Park. Of particular interest to coast walkers is the Old Whaling Station, a boarding house for whalers in the 1850s, and the Allen Knight Maritime Museum, which features exhibits of maritime and naval history. One museum highlight is the 1887 Fresnel lens from the Point Sur Lightstation (See Walk #52).

This walk's destination, the Monterey Bay Aquarium, is open daily from 10:00 a.m. to 6:00 p.m. Call for additional information and tickets: (408) 375-3333.

Directions to trailhead: From Highway 1, and from downtown Monterey, signs direct you to "Fisherman's Wharf." There's parking in the muncipal lot at the end of Alvarado Street.

The Walk: Before heading for Fisherman's Wharf, also known as Wharf #1, check out Municipal Wharf, or Wharf #2. This utilitarian structure, built in 1926, serves Monterey's commercial fishing fleet. Cranes, hoists, and forklifts unload the fleet's catch, which can include squid, shrimp, salmon, sole, anchovy and Pacific herring.

Built in 1870 by the Pacific Coast Steamship Company to serve cargo schooners, Fisherman's Wharf became a bustling adjunct to the canneries of Cannery Row during the 1930s. If you walk past the tourist shops, fish markets, and seafood restaurants, you can see sea lions frolicking below the pier. Beware of sea gulls flying overhead; they compete for the fish that tourists throw to the overfed sea lions and pelicans.

Before heading around the bay to Cannery Row, detour across the plaza adjacent the wharf and stop by the Custom House, the oldest public building on the California coast.

When Mexico ruled California, custom duties were collected from foreign ships. The building now houses a collection of clothing, leather goods and china—items typical of what was imported through the port of old Monterey.

Touch tidepool, Monterey Bay Aquarium

Proceed through Shoreline Park on the Monterey Recreation Trail, a paved bicycle/pedestrian path that will eventually extend to Asilomar Conference Center in Pacific Grove. The level route follows the old railbed of the Del Monte Express, which from 1879 to 1972 carried passengers from San Francisco to Pebble Beach and Del Monte Lodge.

Stay on the pedestrian path along the waterfront to the Coast Guard Pier at the southeast end of Cannery Row. A rock jetty extending from the end of the pier is a favorite haul-out for sea lions.

The first fish processing plant on what was to become Cannery Row was built in 1902. Canneries packaged food for human consumption. Reduction plants processed sardine by-products into fish meal for animal feed, and into oil, used in manufacturing such things as paint and vitamins.

Peak sardine production was reached in 1945, the year John Steinbeck's "Cannery Row" was published. During the boom, the humble sardine supported an industry that crowded 23 canneries and 19 reduction plants along one mile of shoreline. Marine scientists warned of overfishing and in 1951 the fish all but vanished from California's waters. There is now some evidence to suggest that the sardine may be making a comeback.

Follow Cannery Row past a mix of abandoned canneries, luxury hotels, restaurants, tourist shops, and a bust of John Steinbeck. As Steinbeck, on a return visit many years after the publication of his novel, summed up Cannery Row: "They fish for tourists now."

The $50 million Monterey Bay Aquarium, which opened in 1984, is one of the world's finest. The state of the art exhibits and 100 display tanks are superb. Particularly noteworthy for admirers of the California coast, is the fact that almost all of displays emphasize the rich underwater world of Monterey Bay.

One aquarium highlight is a mature kelp forest. A multitude of fish swim past tall stands of giant kelp, one of the world's fastest growing plants. Another absorbing exhibit is the Monterey Bay Tank, which recreates the world of one of the world's largest submarine canyons, complete with sharks and brightly colored fish.

Beyond the aquarium, the Monterey Recreation Trail leads past rows of Victorian houses to the wind-sculpted cypress trees atop Lover's Point. From the point's grassy picnic area, you can enjoy a great view of the southern sweep of Monterey Bay.

A towering kelp forest thrives in the 335,000 gallon tank.

58

Loma Prieta Grade Trail

Porter Picnic Area to China Camp: 6 miles round trip; 400-foot gain

One of the largest state parks in central California, The Forest of Nisene Marks, has few facilities, but this very lack of development makes it attractive to anyone looking for a quiet walk in the woods.

The woods, in this case, are second-growth redwoods. The park is on land which was clear-cut during a lumber boom lasting from 1883-1923. Loma Prieta Lumber Company had quite an operation. Using steam engines, oxen, skid roads, and even a railway, loggers ventured into nearly every narrow canyon of the Aptos Creek watershed.

After the Loma Prieta Lumber Company left Aptos Canyon, the forest began to regenerate, and today a handsome, second generation of redwoods is rising to cover the scarred slopes.

The Marks, a prominent Salinas Valley farm family, purchased the land in the 1950s; in 1963, the three Marks children donated the property to the state in the name of their mother, Nisene Marks. As specified in the deed, the forest must not be developed, and the natural process of regeneration must be allowed to continue.

Ferocious winter storms of 1982 and 1983 battered the canyons and ruined part of the park's trail system, in particular, paths in the upper reaches of Aptos Canyon. Railroad grades and trestles that had withstood a century of storms, were washed away. Volunteers and the California Conservation Corps, have since repaired some of the damage.

Loma Prieta Grade Trail follows parts of an old railway bed. A narrow-gauge steam railway ran from a mill to China Camp. A few ramshackle wooden buildings are all that's left of this turn-of-the-century lumber camp that once housed 300 workers.

Directions to trailhead: From Highway 1 in Aptos, exit on Soquel Drive (this road, like Highway 1 at this point, is running east-west) and head west a short distance. Turn right on Aptos Creek Road, and drive four miles to a locked gate at the state park's Porter picnic area.

The Walk: From the picnic area, follow Aptos Creek Road 4/10 mile to the Loma Prieta Grade Trailhead. (The old mill site is a short walk up the road.)

For a short stretch, the trail stays near Aptos Creek. The creek arises high on Santa Rosalia Ridge, is joined by the waters of Bridge Creek, and spills into Monterey Bay at Rio Del Mar Beach. Silver salmon and steelhead spawn in the creek.

The old railway bed makes a gentle trail, except for a few places where the old bridges have collapsed into steep ravines. Your destination of China Camp, now called Hoffman's Historic Site, has a few wooden structures.

You may return the same way, or take the Ridge Connection Trail over to West Ridge Trail. This latter trail runs south and connects with Aptos Creek Road. Be warned that this trail is crowded by profligate amounts of poison oak.

(Left) Youth Conservation Corps works to repair storm-damaged trail.

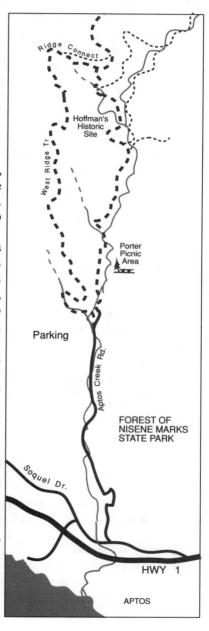

59

Henry Cowell Redwoods Trail

Picnic Area to Observation Deck via River Trail, Eagle Creek Trail,
and Pine Trail;
return via Ridge Trail: 4 miles round trip;
500-foot elevation gain

Henry Cowell Redwoods State Park preserves first- and second-growth redwoods in a tranquil Santa Cruz Mountains setting.

Henry Cowell and Joseph Welch, who in the 1860s acquired the former Mexican land grant Rancho Canada de Rincon, shared a similar commitment to protect the Big Trees Grove (now Redwood Grove). Welch's holdings were purchased by Santa Cruz County in 1930 and became parkland; in the 1950s this land was combined with 1,500 acres donated by Cowell's heirs to become a state park.

Thanks to the preservation efforts by these men, the "Big Trees" are as stirring a sight now as they were a century ago when railroad passengers bound for Santa Cruz from San Jose made a lunch stop amongst the tall trees.

The short Redwood Grove Nature Trail, which visits one of the finest first growth groves south of San Francisco, is a good place to start your exploration of the Santa Cruz Mountains. This popular trail, complete with interpretive leaflet, loops along the San Lorenzo Riverbank among the redwoods, some of which have been given names. One of the larger commemorative redwoods honors President Theodore Roosevelt, who enjoyed his 1903 visit to the grove.

The state park is hilly and with changes in elevation come changes in vegetation. Moisture-loving redwoods predominate on the lowlands while the park's upper ridges are cloaked with oak woodland and chaparral.

By connecting four of the park's trails, you can walk through all of the park's diverse ecosystems. You'll begin in the redwoods and ascend chaparral-covered slopes to an observation deck located in the middle of the park. Great mountain and coastal views are your reward for the ascent.

Be sure to stop in at the park interpretive center, which has exhibits and sells maps and books. Redwood Grove Nature Trail begins near the center.

Directions to trailhead: Henry Cowell Redwoods State Park is located just south of Felton on Highway 9. You can pick up River Trail near the park entrance at Highway 9, or from the picnic area. There is a state park day use fee.

The Walk: River Trail meanders down river along the east bank of the San Lorenzo. You may hear the whistle of the Roaring Camp & Big Trees Railroad, a popular tourist attraction located adjacent to the park. The steam-powered train takes passengers through the Santa Cruz Mountains on narrow gauge track that climbs some of the steepest grades in America.

About a quarter-mile after River Trail passes beneath a Southern Pacific railroad trestle, you'll intersect Eagle Creek Trail and begin ascending out of the redwood forest along Eagle Creek. Madrone and manzanita predominate on the exposed sunny slopes.

Bear right on Pine Trail. The pines you'll see en route are ponderosa pine. You'll pass through the park's campground, rejoin the trail, and climb steeply up to the observation deck. Enjoy the view of the Monterey and Santa Cruz coastline, the redwood forests, and that tumbled-up range of mountains called Santa Cruz.

On the return trip, take Ridge Trail on a steep descent to River Trail. Both River Trail and its nearly parallel path—Pipeline Road—lead back to Redwood Grove and the picnic area.

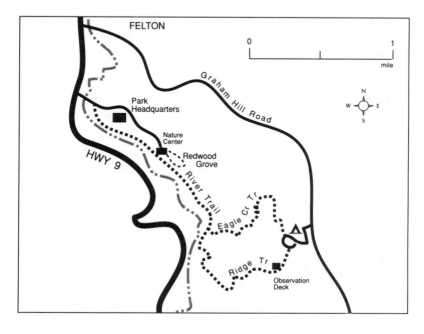

159

60

Monarch Trail

Visitors Center-Nature Trail-Monterey pines: 3/4 mile round trip

Until October, 1989, it was easy to understand why the beach here is called Natural Bridges State Beach. The remaining offshore sandstone bridge stood until the Loma Preita earthquake, centered nearby, caused its collapse. But this park on the outskirts of Santa Cruz still offers plenty of other natural attractions. A eucalyptus grove in the center of the park hosts the largest concentration of monarch butterflies in America. The park has an extensive interpretive program from October through March, when the monarchs winter at the grove.

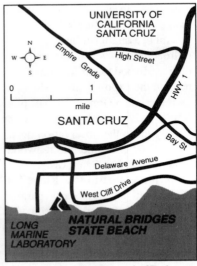

After you explore the park, visit nearby Long Marine Laboratory, located just up-coast at the end of Delaware Avenue. University of California Santa Cruz faculty and students use the research facility, which studies coastal ecology. The lab's Marine Aquarium is open to the public by docent tours 1 to 4 p.m. Tuesday through Sunday.

Directions to trailhead: Natural Bridges State Beach is located off Highway 1 in Santa Cruz at 2531 W. Cliff Drive. Follow the signs from Highway 1. There is a state park day use fee if you bring your vehicle into the park.

The Walk: The signed Monarch Trail begins near the park's small interpretive center. Soon the trail splits; the leftward fork leads to a Monarch observation platform. Sometimes on cold mornings, the butterflies look like small, brown, fluttering leaves. As the sun warms the tropical insects, the "leaves" come to life—bobbing and darting. During spring and summer, the monarchs—easily the country's most recognized butterfly—leave their coastal California birthplace and disperse across America. Winters, however, are spent on the frost-free California coast—from Santa Cruz to Southern California to northern Baja. As many as 200,000 monarchs cluster

Pioneer coast walkers enjoy outing on natural bridge

in the state park on a "good" butterfly year.

The other branch of the trail is a self-guided nature trail. It ends in a grove of Monterey pine.

When you head back to the visitors center, detour down to the beach. Just up the beach is Secret Lagoon, the domain of ducks and great blue herons. Farther up the beach is one of the central coast's truly superb tidepool areas.

61

Skyline to the Sea Trail

*Big Basin Redwoods State Park to Waddell Beach:
11 miles one way; 1,200-foot loss*

Skyline to the Sea Trail, as its name suggests, drops from the crest of the Santa Cruz Mountains to the Pacific. For the most part, it runs downhill on its scenic 38-mile journey from Castle Rock State Park to Big Basin Redwoods State Park to Waddell State Beach. Views from the Skyline—redwood-forested slopes, fern-smothered canyons, and the great blue Pacific—are superb.

This gem of a trail has many friends. During one weekend in 1969, dedicated members of the Sempervirens Fund and the Santa Cruz Trails Association turned out more than two thousand volunteers to dig, clear, prune, and otherwise improve the trail. Area volunteers put together an annual "Trails Day" that is a model for trails organizations around the state.

The wildest and most beautiful part of the Skyline stretches from park headquarters at Big Basin to the Waddell Creek Beach and Marsh. It winds through deep woods, and explores the moist environments of Waddell and Berry Creeks. Springtime, when Berry Creek and Waddell Creek are frothy torrents, and when Berry Creek Falls cascades at full vigor, is a particularly dramatic time to walk the Skyline to the Sea Trail.

You can enjoy the Skyline to the Sea Trail either by following the one-way route described below, or by joining Sunset Trail for a 12-mile loop.

Berry Creek Falls

Directions to trailhead: From Santa Cruz, drive twelve miles north on Highway 9. Turn west on Highway 236 and follow it to the park.

If you're hiking from Big Basin to the sea, you'll need to arrange a car shuttle. Waddell Beach, at trail's end, is located 18 miles up-coast from Santa Cruz.

Better yet, take the bus, which stops at both Big Basin and Waddell Beach. For more information, call the Santa Cruz Metropolitan Transit District: (408) 425-8600.

The Walk: The trail begins in the nucleus of the park on the Opal Creek flatlands at the bottom of the basin. From park headquarters, the trail climbs out of the basin and soon passes junctions with Howard King Trail and trails connecting to Sunset Trail.

The trail descends through deep and dark woods, first with Kelly Creek, then with the west fork of Waddell Creek. Ferns and mushrooms, salamanders and banana slugs, occupy the wet world of the trail.

Some four miles from the trailhead, just short of the confluence of Waddell Creek and Berry Creek, you'll intersect Berry Creek Falls Trail. The falls cascade over fern-covered cliffs into a frothy pool. An ideal lunch stop, or turnaround spot, is Sunset Trail Camp, located a mile up Berry Creek Falls Trail, and near another falls—Golden Falls.

Skyline to the Sea Trail descends with Waddell Creek and passes through the heart of the beautiful Waddell Valley. Rancho del Oso, "Ranch of the Bears," as this region is known, has second-generation redwoods, Douglas fir, Monterey pine, as well as lush meadows.

In 1914, mining engineer Theodore Hoover purchased a good part of Waddell Valley. He and his descendants preserved the natural beauty of the area and encouraged natural history studies. Now that the valley is part of the state park, rangers and volunteers conduct nature study activities at Rancho del Oso Nature and History Center.

A mile and a half from the ocean, you'll reach Twin Redwoods Camp. As you near the sea, the redwoods give way to laurel groves and meadow land. Near trail's end is a freshwater marsh, a favorite stopping place for migratory birds on the Pacific flyway. A wildlife sanctuary, Theodore J. Hoover Natural Preserve, has been established in the heart of the marsh area to protect the over two hundred kinds of native and migatory birds that reside or visit this valuable habitat.

The trail ends at Highway 1. West of the highway is a bus stop and windswept Waddell Beach.

62

Ano Nuevo Trail

3 miles round trip

One of the best new year's resolutions a walker could make is to plan a winter trip to Ano Nuevo State Reserve. Here you'll be treated to a wildlife drama that attracts visitors from all over the world—a close-up look at the largest mainland population of elephant seals.

From December through April, a colony of the huge creatures visits Ano Nuevo Island and Point in order to breed and bear young. To protect the elephant seals (and the humans who hike out to see them), the Reserve is open only through naturalist-guided tours during these months.

Slaughtered for their oil-rich blubber, the elephant seal population numbered less than one hundred by the turn of the century. Placed under government protection, the huge mammals rebounded rapidly from the brink of extinction. Ano Nuevo State Reserve was created in 1958 to protect the seals.

Male elephant seals, some reaching lengths of 16 feet and weighing 3 tons, arrive in December and begin battling for dominance. Only a very small percentage of males actually get to inseminate a female; most remain lifelong bachelors. The females, relatively svelte at 1,200 to 2,000 pounds, come ashore in January and join the harems of the dominant males.

La Punta De Ano Nuevo (The Point of the New Year) was named by the Spanish explorer Vizcaino on January 3, 1603. It's one of the oldest place-names in California.

At the time of its discovery, the Point was occupied by Ohlone Indians, who lived off the bounty of sea. Judging from kitchen midden sites—shell mounds—found in the nearby dunes, it was a rich bounty indeed.

The Ano Nuevo area later hosted a variety of enterprises. From the 1850s to 1920, redwood cut from the slopes of the nearby Santa Cruz Mountains was shipped from Ano Nuevo Bay. A dairy industry flourished on the coastal bluffs. The Reserve's visitors center is a restored century- old dairy barn.

While the elephant seals are clearly the main attraction when they come ashore during the winter to breed and during the summer to molt, the Reserve is even fascinating when the seals are not in residence. Bird-watchers may glimpse a cliff swallow, western gull, red-tailed hawk and many other inland and shore birds. Joining the elephant seals on Ano Nuevo Island are Steller sea lions, California sea lions and harbor seals. The beautiful sand dunes of

Bull elephant seals negotiate territorial rights

the Reserve are covered with beach grass, morning glory and extensive patches of beach strawberry.

Directions to trailhead: Ano Nuevo State Reserve is located just west of Highway 1, 20 miles north of Santa Cruz and 30 miles south of Half Moon Bay.

Reservations/ Information: Ano Nuevo Point, where the elephant seals reside, is open only to visitors on guided walks, which are conducted by park volunteers and by volunteer docents of the Ano Nuevo Interpretive Association. Guided walks are conducted daily and consist of a 2 1/2 hour, three-mile long walk.

Advance reservations for the guided walks are strongly recommended. Reservations can be made at Ticketron outlets. You can also use VISA and Mastercard to make a reservation by phoning Ticketron's Teletron numbers. If you reserve your tickets by phone, a handling surcharge is added to the ticket price.

For more information about Ano Nuevo State Reserve: (415) 879-0227.

Guided tours along the 3-mile trail are available for disabled persons. For details: (415) 879-0454, Tuesday through Friday.

In addition, another, shorter trail designed by state park ranger Nina Gordon, will accomodate wheelchairs. Gordon's trail utilizes heavy rubber matting in order to provide the firm surface needed for wheelchairs to cross the reserve's shifting sand dunes. Call the park for more information.

63

Butano Loop Trail

Mill Ox Trail, Goat Hill Trail, Ano Nuevo Trail:
4 miles round trip; 700-foot gain

According to local Indian lore, Butano means "a gathering place for friendly visits." Visitors who find out-of-the-way Butano State Park will no doubt agree with the Indians' assessment.

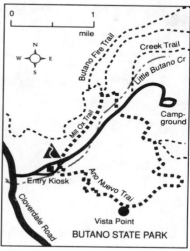

On the map, Butano State Park seems rather close to the bustling Santa Clara Valley, and to the Bay area. But this 2,200-acre park, tucked between sharp, Santa Cruz Mountains ridges, has a remote feeling. This feeling of remoteness is heightened by a twenty-mile trail network that leads through redwoods and a fern canyon, as well as climbing to some great vista points.

While most of the redwoods in the park are second-growth, some grand old first-growth specimens remain. The land was logged during the 1880s, but did not endure the devastating clearcuts common to other coastal ridges of the Santa Cruz Mountains. The steep terrain nixed conventional transportation, so the woodsmen had to settle for cutting shakes, posts, and fence rails—products that could be more easily hauled to market.

On lower slopes, just above Butano Creek, the walker encounters the forest primeval: redwoods, trillium, sword ferns. Moss-draped Douglas fir, tangles of blackberry bushes, and meadowland, are some of the environments visited by the park's diverse trail system. Ano Nuevo Lookout offers fine views of the elephant seal reserve, and of the San Mateo coastline.

Directions to trailhead: From Highway 1, turn inland on Pescadero Road, and drive 2 1/2 miles to Cloverdale Road. Drive south 3 miles to Butano State Park Road and turn left into the park. Leave your car near the entry kiosk.

Waiting out the rain, a frequent occurence in the Santa Cruz Mountains

The Walk: Signed Jackson Flats Trail begins just across from the park entry kiosk. The path starts out in meadowland, but soon enters redwoods. The trail follows the north slope of the canyon cut by Little Butano Creek, and junctions with Mill Ox Trail.

Take Mill Ox Trail to the right, down to the canyon bottom. Cross Butano State Park Road, and join an unmarked (except for an "authorized vehicles only" sign) paved road. Ascend through redwoods on this access road. The route soon junctions with Goat Hill Trail, which you follow into a mixed forest of oak and madrone. Follow this trail to the next intersection: Goat Hill Trail heads left and melts into the woods, but you take the short connector path to Olmo Fire Trail. Turn right.

Olmo Fire Trail leads to a junction with Ano Nuevo Trail on your left. Take this path over fir- and blackberry bush-covered slopes to Ano Nuevo Viewpoint, located in a clearing. You can look south to Ano Nuevo Island, the sea elephant rookery.

From the viewpoint, the trail descends, with enough switchbacks to make a snake dizzy, back to the park entrance.

64

Pescadero Marsh Trails

Pescadero State Beach to North Marsh: 2 1/2 miles round trip
Pescadero State Beach to North Pond (closed 3/15 to 9/1):
*   2 1/2 miles round trip*
West Butano Loop: 1 3/4 miles round trip

Bring a pair of binoculars to Pescadero Marsh Natural Preserve, the largest marsh between Monterey Bay and San Francisco. Pescadero Creek and Butano Creek pool resources to form a lagoon and estuary that is a haven for birds, and a heaven for bird-watchers.

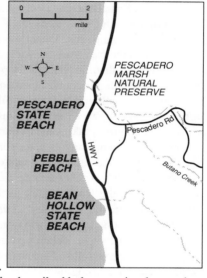

Peer through the willows, tules, and cattails, and you might spot diving ducks, great egrets, or yellow-throated warblers. More than 180 species of birds have been sighted in the preserve.

Best bird-watching is during the late fall and early spring. To protect the birds during breeding season, the northernmost preserve trail is closed.

You may take one of the three walks described below, or simply wander the perimeter of the marsh to one of the wooden observation decks, and begin your bird-watching.

Directions to trailhead: Pescadero State Beach and Pescadero Marsh Natural Preserve are located off Highway 1, some 15 miles south of Half Moon Bay. The state beach has three parking areas. The largest area is at the south end of the beach, where Pescadero Road junctions Highway 1.

The Walk: From the southernmost state beach parking area, follow the beach north. If it's low tide, you'll get a good look at some fascinating tidepools.

A half-mile of travel brings you to the mouth of Butano Creek. You may have to hike inland a bit to find a good place to ford the creek.

Turn inland and pass under the highway bridge. You'll join Sequoia

Audubon Trail, which meanders between the south shore of North Marsh and the north bank of Butano Creek. Take the first fork to the left and loop toward North Marsh. A right turn, as you near the marsh, will allow you to loop back to the Sequoia Audubon Trail.

To North Pond: (closed 3/15-9/1) Walk north on Pescadero Beach. A half-mile beyond Butano Creek, you'll come to the massive cliff faces of San Mateo Coast State Beaches. (With a low tide, you could walk along the base of the cliffs to San Gregorio Beach.) Turn inland to the northern Pescadero State Beach parking area. Directly across the road from the entrance to the parking lot is the trailhead for North Marsh Trail.

Follow the half-mile path as it loops around North Pond. Cattle graze the slopes above the pond, and abundant birdlife populates the surrounding thickets. The path climbs a small hill where a wooden observation deck affords a grand view of the large North Marsh.

You can return by taking the trail south and to the left. It leads to Sequoia Audubon Trail, which in turn takes you under the Butano Creek Bridge. You then follow the beach back to your starting point.

West Butano Loop: For another fine bird walk, transport yourself a half-mile up Pescadero Road. Entry to the small, dirt parking area is almost directly opposite the San Mateo County road maintenance station.

The unsigned trail leads north from the parking area, and winds through a wide, lush meadow. When you get to the creek, follow the trail east (rightward). As you follow Butano Creek, you'll be walking the tops of dikes which once allowed coastal farmers to use this rich bottom land for growing artichokes, brussels sprouts, and beans. Adjacent lands are still carefully cultivated by local farmers.

Watch for blue herons and snowy egrets. Perhaps you'll even spot the San Francisco garter snake, an endangered species. After following Butano Creek through the marsh, you'll join the trail to the right to return to the starting point.

65

Arroyo de los Frijoles Trail

Pebble Beach to Bean Hollow Beach: 2 miles round trip

Pebble Beach—not to be confused with the Pebble Beach of 18-hole renown near Carmel, the Pebble Beach in Tomales Bay State Park, or the Pebble Beach near Crescent City—is one of those enchanting San Mateo County beaches that extend from Ano Nuevo State Reserve to Thornton State Beach, a bit south of San Francisco. The pebbles on the beach are quartz chipped from an offshore reef, tumbled ashore, then wave-polished and rounded into beautifully hued small stones.

The one-mile walk between Pebble Beach and Bean Hollow Beach offers a close-up look at tidepools, wildflowers (in season), and colonies of harbor seals and shorebirds.

Directions to trailhead: Pebble Beach is located some 40 miles south of San Francisco. The beach is off Highway 1, about 2 1/2 miles south of Pescadero. The trail begins at the south end of the parking lot.

The Walk: Some walkers say that the San Mateo County beaches and bluffs remind them of the British coast near Cornwall. This comparison is reinforced at the beginning of the trail, which crosses a moor-like environment bedecked with iris and daisies.

The first part of the walk is along a nature trail, which is keyed to an interpretive brochure that apparently fell victim to state park interpretive program cutbacks.

Waves crashing over the offshore reef are a dramatic sight. Keep an eye out for harbor seals swimming just offshore.

The rocky intertidal area is habitat for sea slugs and snails, anenomes and urchins. Bird-watchers will sight cormorants, pelicans and red-billed oyster catchers flying over the water. The sandy beach is patrolled by gulls, sandpipers and sanderlings.

A couple of small foot bridges aid your crossing of rivulets that carve the coastal bluffs. To the south, you'll get a glimpse of Pigeon Point Lighthouse, now part of a hostel. If the tide is low when you approach Bean Hollow State Beach, head down to the sand.

Arroyo de los Frijoles, "Creek of the Beans," empties into Lake Lucerne, just east of Pacific Coast Highway. The state beach originally had the Spanish name before being Americanized to Bean Hollow. Picnic tables at the beach suggest a lunch or rest stop.

▲ 66
Sweeney Ridge

Pacifica to San Francisco Bay Discovery Site:
3 1/2 miles round trip; 600-foot gain

Unlike most California coastal locales, San Francisco Bay was discovered by walkers, not sailors. The bay's infamous fog, and its narrow opening, had concealed it from passing ships for two centuries when Captain Gaspar de Portola sighted it on November 4, 1769.

The actual discovery site is atop Sweeney Ridge above the town of Pacifica. Portola was, at first, miffed by his discovery because he realized that his expedition had overshot its intended destination of Monterey Bay. He soon realized, however, that he had discovered one of the world's great natural harbors, and he figured it would be an ideal place for his government to build another presidio. Portola's discovery aided Captain Ayala, who was then able to sail his San Carlos into the bay.

It was quite a conservation battle to save Sweeney Ridge. The late Congressman Phillip Burton, aided by many bay area conservationists, succeeded in placing a thousand acres of the ridgetop under the protection of the Golden Gate National Recreation Area.

Sweeney Ridge is the name of the trail you'll use while walking the ridge itself. Four trails lead to Sweeney Ridge: Baquiano Trail and Mori Ridge Trail lead eastward to Portola's discovery site, while Sneath Lane Trail and Skyline College Trail climb southward to the ridgetop.

172

Directions to trailhead: Mori Ridge: From Highway 1 at the outskirts of Pacifica, turn east at the first opportunity south of Fairway Drive. You'll see a sign: Shelldance Exotic Plant Nursery. Take this road 3/10 of a mile to its end and park near the nursery.

Fassler Avenue: Take Highway 1 to the Rockaway Beach area of Pacifica. Follow Fassler eastbound to its end at a gate.

Skyline College: Take Highway 35 to San Bruno. Turn west on College Drive, following it to the south side of campus. Look for parking area #2.

Sneath Lane: Take highways 280 or 35 to Sneath Lane exit in San Bruno. Follow the lane westbound to the end at Sweeney Ridge.

The Walk: The ridge is often cloaked in morning fog, and in the afternoon, the wind really kicks up. When it's foggy, the coastal scrub and grasslands are bathed in a strange, sharp light. Sweeney Ridge is particularly attractive in spring, when lupine, poppies, cream cups, and gold fields color the slopes.

And the view is magnificent: Mount Tam and Mount Diablo, the Golden Gate and the Farallon Islands, plus dozens of communities clustered around the bay.

Gaspar de Portola sighted San Francisco Bay, from what we now call Sweeney Ridge, in 1769

173

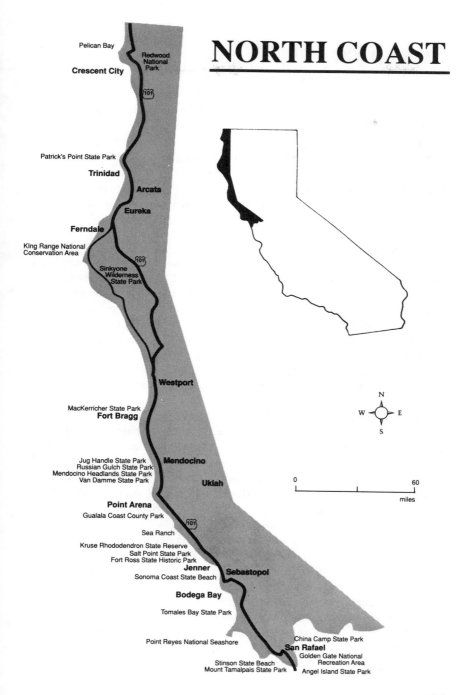

NORTH COAST

Pelican Bay

Redwood National Park

Crescent City

101

Patrick's Point State Park

Trinidad

Arcata

Eureka

Ferndale

King Range National Conservation Area

101

Sinkyone Wilderness State Park

Westport

MacKerricher State Park
Fort Bragg

Jug Handle State Park
Russian Gulch State Park
Mendocino Headlands State Park
Van Damme State Park

Mendocino

Ukiah

Point Arena

Gualala Coast County Park

101

Sea Ranch

Kruse Rhododendron State Reserve
Salt Point State Park
Fort Ross State Historic Park

Jenner

Sebastopol

Sonoma Coast State Beach

Bodega Bay

Tomales Bay State Park

China Camp State Park

Point Reyes National Seashore

San Rafael

Golden Gate National Recreation Area

Stinson State Beach
Mount Tamalpais State Park

Angel Island State Park

N
W — E
S

0   60
miles

175

NORTH COAST

San Francisco is a city of walkers. And many of the city's best walks are coast walks along the bay and ocean shores of the Golden Gate National Recreation Area. GGNRA, as it's known, extends across the Golden Gate Bridge, and protects the wild headlands of Marin County.

From the "Bridge at the Edge of the Continent," walkers are treated to splendorous views of San Francisco Bay, which contains ninety per cent of California's remaining coastal wetlands. Other great bay views—and great walks—can be had from China Camp State Park, Angel Island and Mount Tamalpais.

The Bay Area is rich in coastal trails. An officially-designated Coast Trail heads through Golden Gate National Recreation Area, Mount Tamalpais State Park, and 71,000-acre Pt. Reyes National Seashore. Coast Trail offers days and weekends of fine hiking to remote backcountry camps.

Pt. Reyes National Seashore, with its densely forested ridges, wild and open coastal bluffs, and deserted beaches, is an unforgettable place to ramble. With its moors, weirs, glens and vales, Pt. Reyes Peninsula calls to mind the seacoast of Great Britain. When the fog settles over the dew-dampened grasslands of Tomales Point, walkers can easily imagine that they're stepping onto a Scottish moor, or wandering one of the Shetland Islands.

North of Marin County are Sonoma and Mendocino County, sometimes called Mendoma, a sparsely populated and little developed coastline. As you travel north, you pass from rolling grass-covered hillsides and broad marine terraces to steep cliffs and densely forested coastal mountains.

The names on Sonoma's shore are intriguing: Blind Beach and Schoolhouse Beach, Arched Rock and Goat Rock, Penny Island and Bodega Head. These colorfully-named locales are the highlight of Sonoma Coast State Beach, which is not one beach, but many.

In Mendocino County, at Van Damme and Russian Gulch State Parks, another very special environment awaits the walker: the Pygmy Forest. A nutrient-poor, highly acidic topsoil has severely restricted the growth of trees to truly Lilliputian size. Sixty-year old cypress trees are but a few feet tall and measure a half inch in diameter.

Few coastal locales are as photographed as the town of Mendocino and its bold headlands. The town itself, which lies just north of the mouth of Big River, resembles a New England village. Now protected by a state park, the Mendocino Headlands are laced with trails that offer postcard views of wave

tunnels and tidepools, beaches and blowholes.

Sinkyone Wilderness State Park and King Range National Conservation Area are part of California's famed Lost Coast— an area of unstable earth and fast-rising mountains. The San Andreas Fault lies just offshore and touches land at Shelter Cove. So rugged is this country, highway engineers were forced to route Highway 1 many miles inland, and the region has remained sparsely settled and unspoiled. Its magnificent vistas and varied terrain—dense forests, prairies, and black sand beaches—reward the hearty explorer.

California's coastline rises to a magnificent crescendo at Redwood National Park. Redwood Creek Trail travels through the heart of the national park to Tall Trees Grove, site of the world's tallest tree.

The redwoods seem most at home in places like Gold Bluffs, in Prairie Creek Redwoods State Park. Dim and quiet, wrapped in mist and silence, the redwoods roof a moist and mysterious world.

Many beautiful "fern canyons" are found along the north coast. The one in Prairie Creek Redwoods State Park is particularly awe-inspiring. Bracken, five-finger, lady, sword, and chain ferns smother the precipitous walls of the canyon.

Lucky walkers might catch a glimpse of the herd of Roosevelt elk that roam the state park. These graceful animals look like a cross between a South American llama and a deer and convince (if any convincing is necessary) walkers that they have indeed entered an enchanted land.

▲ 67
Coastal Trail

Cliff House to Golden Gate Bridge: 6 miles round trip

San Francisco is known as a city of walkers. Whether this reputation is due to its relatively healthy, vigorous, upscale population, or to the city's terrible traffic and paucity of parking, is open for debate.

Some of the city's best walks are coast walks, which explore the northern and western edges of San Francisco's shoreline. A good part of this shoreline is under the jurisdiction of Golden Gate National Recreation Area. An intrepid walker could explore much of the urban shoreline of the recreation area in one long day. One could begin at Fort Funston, walk along Ocean Beach, visit Cliff House, Land's End, Baker Beach, Fort Point and the Golden Gate. The tireless walker could then continue along the city's north shore, heading bayside past Crissy Field, and heading along Golden Promenade to park headquarters and Fort Mason.

This walk, a scenic and historic journey from Cliff House to the Golden Gate, explores a portion of San Francisco's diverse shoreline.

Today's Cliff House, perched above Ocean Beach, is the third structure erected on this site. In 1863, the first roadhouse was built; it catered to the wealthy, high-toned carriage crowd. Along came millionaire and philanthropist Adolph Sutro, who had moved to San Francisco after making his fortune as an engineer during Nevada's silverstrike era. Sutro thought that the city's working class residents would enjoy a seaside diversion. He built

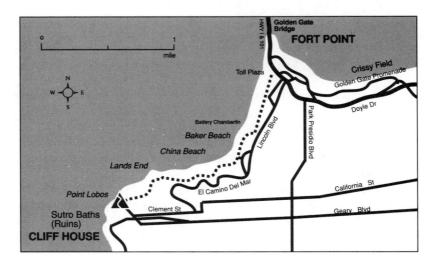

a steam railway from downtown to the coast; the ride to Cliff House cost a nickel.

The original Cliff House, called Seal Rock House, burned. Sutro replaced it with a six-story gingerbread-style Victorian mansion. This, too, burned in 1907. Sutro again rebuilt, this time building a more utilitarian structure— more or less the one you see today.

The present Cliff House includes a gift shop, restaurant, Musee Mechanique, full of coin-operated games, and the Camera Obscura. There's a GGNRA information center and a great collection of historic photographs and exhibits.

Directions to trailhead: From Highway 101 (Van Ness Boulevard) in the city, turn west on Geary Boulevard and follow it to its end. As the road turns south toward Ocean Beach, you'll see Cliff House on your right.

Remains of Sutro Baths

The Walk: From the Cliff House balcony, enjoy the view of Seal Rocks, frequented by seals and noisy sea lions. After you've enjoyed the many attractions of Cliff House, walk northeast a short distance to Greco-Roman-like ruins of the Sutro Baths. Six saltwater swimming pools and a freshwater plunge were heated by a complex series of pipes and canals. Museums, galleries and restaurants were also part of the complex built by Adolph Sutro in 1890. The popularity of public spas gradually waned and, in 1966, fire destroyed all but the cement foundations of the baths.

From the baths, wander north over to the Merrie Way parking area and pick up the Coastal Trail. You'll begin walking on the abandoned railroad bed of the old Cliff House and Ferries Railroad. The trail winds through cypress and coastal sage, and hugs the cliffs below El Camino del Mar.

179

Coastal Trail leads along the Lincoln Park Bluffs. If its low tide when you look down at the shoreline, you might be able to spot the wreckage of some of the ships that have been dashed to pieces on the rocks below. This rocky, precipitous stretch of coast is known as Land's End.

You'll get great views from the Eagle Point Lookout, then briefly join El Camino Del Mar through the wealthy Seacliff residential area. A quarter-mile of travel (keep bearing left) brings you to sandy China Beach, once a turn- of-the-century encampment for Chinese fishermen. The beach is also known as James Phelan Beach for the politician/philanthropist, who left part of his fortune to help California writers and artists.

Backtrack to Sea Cliff Avenue, following the westernmost lanes of this fancy residential area, and continue north a short half-mile to expansive Baker Beach. At the south end of the beach is the outlet of Lobos Creek. In his autobiography, Ansel Adams recalled the many delightful days he spent as a child exploring Lobos Creek. These childhood adventures were the great photographer's first contact with the natural world.

At the north end of Baker Beach is Battery Chamberlain, a former coastal defense site, complete with a "disappearing" 95,000-pound cannon. On weekends, park rangers demonstrate how the cannon could be cranked into its cement, tree-hidden bunker.

Follow the beach service road up through the cypress to Lincoln Boulevard. Coast Trail is a bit indistinct as it follows the boulevard's guard rail for a half-mile of contouring along the coastal cliffs. The trail meanders among cypress and passes more military installations— Batteries Crosby, Dynamite, and Marcus Miller. Beyond the last battery, Coast Trail leads under the Golden Gate Bridge. Just after the trail passes under the bridge, you can follow a path to historic Fort Point.

Fishermen try their luck from Seal Rock

▲ 68
Golden Gate Trail

Fort Point to Vista Point: 3 miles round trip

It's known as one of the world's engineering marvels, the proud emblem of a proud city, and "The Bridge at the End of the Continent." The Golden Gate is all of this—and a great walk: one of those must-do-once-in-a-lifetime adventures.

The technically-inclined revel in the bridge's vital statistics: its 8,981-foot length, cables that support 200 million pounds, twin towers the height of 65-story buildings. Statisticians have calculated everything from the number of gallons of International Orange paint required to cover 10 million square feet of bridge, to the number of star-crossed lovers who have leaped from bridge to bay.

For all its utilitarian value, the bridge is also an artistic triumph. As you walk the bridge, try to remember how many set-in-San Francisco movies and television shows have opened with an establishing shot of the bridge.

The bridge spans 400 square miles of San Francisco Bay, which is really three bays—San Francisco and the smaller San Pablo and Suisun Bays to the north and northeast. Geographers describe the bay as the drowned mouth and floodplain of the Sacramento-San Joaquin Rivers.

Ninety percent of California's remaining coastal wetlands are contained in San Francisco Bay and its estuaries. Shoreline development and industrial pollutants have damaged fish, shellfish, and bird populations; fortunately, a great many people care about the bay, and are working hard to save and rehabilitate one of the state's most important natural resources.

For centuries, high mountains and heavy fogs concealed one of the world's great natural anchorages from passing European ships. It was a coast walker—Seargeant Jose Francisco de Ortega, of the 1769 Portola overland expedition—who first sighted San Francisco Bay. (See Walk #66 up Sweeney Ridge to the San Francisco Bay Discovery Site.) It's possible that Sir Francis Drake sailed his Golden Hinde into the bay two hundred years earlier, but this is a matter of much controversy. (See Walk #75 to Drake's Estero.)

Guarding the Golden Gate is Fort Point, a huge Civil War-era structure built of red brick. The fort, similar in design to Fort Sumter in South Carolina, was built for the then-astronomical cost of $2.8 million, and was intended to ensure California's loyalty to the Union.

Fort Point is now part of Golden Gate National Recreation Area. You'll enjoy prowling the three-story fort's many corridors and stairwells. There

The vision and persistence of engineer Joseph Strauss led to the construction of one of the world's great landmarks

are several fine military exhibits, including one emphasizing the contribution of black American soldiers. From 1933 to 1937, the fort was the coordinating center for the bridge construction.

While the walk across the bridge is unique, and the clear-day views grand, the trip can also be wearing on the nerves. A bone-chilling wind often buffets bridge walkers, and traffic vibrating the bridge also seems to vibrate one's very being. Anyone afraid of heights should walk elsewhere.

To best enjoy the bridge walk, start well away from it, perhaps even as far away as Fisherman's Wharf, Fort Mason, or Marina Green. It's a pleasing bayside stroll past the yacht harbor and Crissy Field, and along Golden Gate Promenade to Fort Point.

Directions to trailhead: Don't try to drive as close as you can to the bridge. First-time visitors invariably miss the view point parking area just south of the toll plaza and before they know it, end up in Sausalito. Fort Point's parking lot is one good place to leave your car, as are other parking lots along the bay.

The Walk: From Fort Point, a gravel, then paved, road leads up to a statue of visionary engineer Joseph Strauss, who persuaded a doubting populace to build the bridge.

As you start walking along the bridge's east sidewalk, you'll get a great view of Fort Point. You'll pause frequently to watch the ship traffic: yachts, tankers, tug boats, ferries, passenger liners. Literally everything necessary for modern life, from California almonds to Japanese cars, passes in and out of the bay by freighter.

Splendorous clear-day views include the cities of the East Bay, and the bold headlands of Marin, which form the more rural part of Golden Gate National Recreation Area. You'll spot Treasure, Alcatraz and Angel Islands, and of course, the San Francisco skyline.

The bridge's second high tower marks the beginning of Marin County. Vista Point is the end of your bridge walk. Here you'll witness tourists from around the world photographing each other and proclaiming their admiration for the Golden Gate in a dozen foreign languages.

69

Angel Island Loop Trail

5 miles round trip: 400-foot gain

For an island barely a square mile in size, Angel Island has an extremely diverse history. Over the last two centuries, the island has seen use as a pirate's supply station, a Mexican land grant, an Army artillery emplacement, and an Immigrant Detention Center. Now it's a state park, attracting hikers, history buffs, and islophiles of all persuasions.

A hundred years of U.S. military occupation began in 1863 when the first gun batteries were installed. The military used the island until 1964, when its Nike Missile Station was deactivated. During wartime periods—particularly during the Spanish-American War—Angel Island was one of the busiest outposts in America. The island served as a processing center for men about to be dispatched to the Philippines, and as a reception/quarantine center for those soldiers who came back with tropical diseases.

Not all of the island's attractions are historical. Rocky coves and sandy beaches, grassy slopes and forested ridges, plus a fine trail network, adds up to a walker's delight. Perimeter Road, takes the walker on a five-mile tour of the island, and offers a different bay view from every turn. From atop Mt. Livermore, a terrific 360-degree panorama unfolds of San Franciso Bay and the Golden Gate.

Directions to trailhead: For information about ferry service, call Angel Island State Park (415) 435-1915; Tiburon Ferry (415) 435-2131; Red and White Fleet (415) 546-2816. The ferries land at Ayala Cove on the northwest side of the island.

Angel, the Bay's largest island

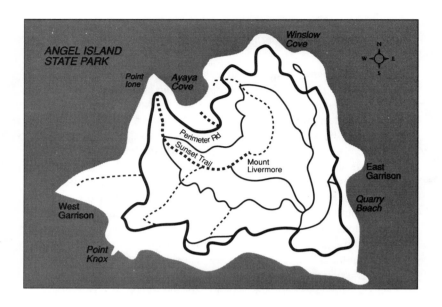

The Walk: When you disembark, head for the park visitors center, located in a white building that once served as bachelor quarters for unmarried officers assigned to the U.S. Quarantine Station that operated here from 1892 to 1949. Ayala Cove was named Hospital Cove then. At the visitors center, you can check out the interpretive exhibits and pick up a park map.

Walk uphill on the road to the left of the visitors center. You'll intersect Perimeter Road, which you'll take to the right. Soon you'll see signed Sunset Trail, on your left.

Sunset Trail switchbacks up steep, coastal-scrub covered slopes, to the top of 781-foot Mt. Caroline Livermore. Picnic tables have replaced the anti-aircraft guns and Nike Missile installation that once stood on the summit. Views of Ayala Cove, Tiburon, and the Golden Gate, are memorable.

Continuing on Perimeter Road, you'll soon be overlooking Camp Reynolds (West Garrison). A side road leads down to the island's first military fortifications. You can walk the parade ground, and see the brick hospital built in 1869. Still standing are the chapel, stables, barracks, and several more structures. Some of the buildings are being restored.

Perimeter Road turns eastward, contouring around ice plant-covered slopes and offering a view down to Point Blunt. You may hear and see the seals gathered around the point.

Continue straight ahead at a four-way intersection. The road curves north and soon arrives at East Garrison, where a collection of utilitarian-looking buildings are a reminder of the many thousands of men who were processed here. East Garrison trained about 30,000 men a year for overseas duty. The hospital, barracks, mess hall, and officers homes, still stand.

Continue north. You'll soon come to the Immigration Station, the so-called "Ellis Island of the West." From 1910 to 1940, 175,000 immigrants, mostly Asians, were (often rudely) processed. During World War II, German, Italian, and Japanese, prisoners of war were confined here.

Perimeter Road rounds Pt. Campbell, northernmost part of the island, and you'll get a glimpse of the Richmond-San Rafael Bridge, and then a view of Tiburon, before the road descends to Ayala Cove.

In the quiet of the night, I heard, faintly,

the whistling of wind.

The forms and shadows saddened me;

upon seeing the landscape, I composed a poem.

The floating clouds, the fog, darkened the sky.

The moon shines faintly as the insects chirp.

Grief and bitterness entwined are heaven sent.

The sad person sits alone, leaning by a window.

Written on the wall by internee, Yu of Taishan, China

70
China Camp Loop Trail

Miwok Trail, Back Ranch Trail,View Point, Ridge Trail:
5 miles round trip; 1,000-foot gain

On Point San Pedro Peninsula, only a few ramshackle buildings remain of the once-thriving shrimp fishing village of China Camp. In the last century, more than thirty such camps were established on the shores of San Francisco Bay. The fishermen were mostly Chinese, who came to America from the city of Canton.

The fishermen staked nets on the shallow bay bottom, in order to capture the tiny grass shrimp. The shrimp were dried, then the meat separated from the shell. It was a labor-intensive process, but a ready market for the shrimp existed in China and Japan.

Competing fishermen helped push through legislation that banned the use of bag nets, and in 1905, the export of dried shrimp was banned entirely, thus ending the San Francisco Bay shrimping business.

In 1977, the state acquired 1,500 acres of bay shore to form China Camp State Park. Some 1890s-era buildings still stand, and interpretive exhibits tell of the difficult life in this fishing village.

After you've absorbed some of the area's colorful history, it's time to explore the state park's backcountry. The park's trail system climbs from Miwok Meadows to forested ridges, and offers fine bay views.

Directions to trailhead: From Highway 101 in San Rafael, take the North San Pedro Road exit, and head east through a residential area to China Camp State Park. Leave your car in one of the parking areas along North San Pedro Road, opposite Miwok Meadows.

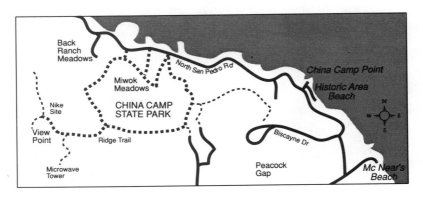

Occasionally a shrimp boat works the waters near historic China Camp

The Walk: Three unsigned, short, spur trails lead south across Miwok Meadows to intersect with Miwok Trail. No matter which spur you take, bear right (west), on Miwok Trail. This path jogs south, becomes Back Ranch Trail, and soon leads to the park's walk-in campground.

From the camp, the trail switchbacks up slopes forested with oak, madrone, and bay. When you pause to catch you breath, look behind you and you'll see the park's four distinct shoreline hills—Jake's Island, Turtle Back, Bullet Hill and Chicken Coop Hill. When bay waters were higher, these hills were islands.

At the intersection with Ridge Trail, you may proceed right (west), up to the former Nike Missile Station. Fine views of San Pablo Bay are yours from this viewpoint.

Heading east, Ridge Trail passes near the community of Glenwood. Two unsigned trails lead rightward into a residential area, but you'll stay left and begin a steep descent on Miwok Trail. This path intersects North San Pedro Road near Chicken Coop Hill.

190

♠ 71
Coast Trail

Tennessee Valley to Tennessee Cove: 4 miles round trip
Tennessee Valley to Muir Beach: 9 miles round trip; 800-foot gain

It was a dark and stormy night...when the side-wheel steamship Tennessee, with 600 passengers aboard, overshot the Golden Gate and ran aground off this isolated Marin County cove. No lives were lost on that foggy night of March 6, 1853, but the abandoned ship was soon broken up by the surf. The Tennessee is remembered by a point, a cove, a valley and a beach.

Although only a few miles north of San Francisco, Tennessee Valley, walled in by high ridges, seems quite isolated from the world. Until 1976 when it became part of the Golden Gate National Recreation Area, the valley was part of the Witter Ranch.

GGNRA's Coast Trail is truly a path of discovery. In San Francisco, it visits many historical attractions sprinkled along the ocean and bay shoreline's of the city. In Marin County, Coast Trail takes walkers over forested ridges, atop rocky cliffs, and down to hidden beaches.

Tennessee Valley Trail junctions with Coast Trail about a half-mile from Tennessee Beach. The walk through Tennessee Valley to the beach is suitable for the whole family. More intrepid walkers will join Coast Trail for an up-and-down journey to Muir Beach.

Coast Trail, Golden Gate National Recreation Area

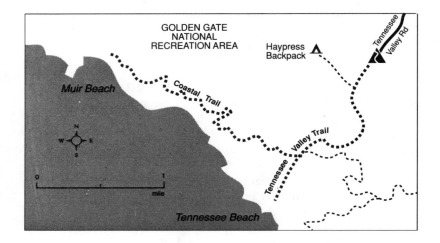

Directions to trailhead: From Highway 101 north of the Golden Gate Bridge, take the Highway 1 offramp. Follow the highway a half-mile, turn left on Tennessee Valley Road, and follow this road to the trailhead and parking area.

The Walk: Tennessee Valley Trail begins as a paved road, farther on becomes gravel, and farther still becomes a footpath. The route descends moderately alongside a willow- and eucalyptus-lined creek, and passes the Tennessee Valley Ranger Station.

About a half-mile from Tennessee Cove, the trail intersects Coast Trail. Continuing on Tennessee Valley Trail will take you past a small lagoon, located just inland from Tennessee Beach. A trail circles the lagoon, and leads back to Tennessee Valley Trail.

Right at the above-mentioned fork will connect you with Coast Trail. As you ascend to the north, pause to look behind you at Tennessee Valley. Coast Trail flattens out for a bit, then descends to Pirate's Cove. The trail marches up and down the coastal bluffs and passes a junction with Coyote Ridge Trail. You'll get a grand view of Muir Beach and Green Gulch. From this junction, you'll descend steeply down to the lagoon formed by Redwood Creek, and to Muir Beach.

192

◭ 72
Steep Ravine Trail

Pantoll to Stinson Beach: 3 miles one-way; 1,100-foot loss

For more than century, Bay Area walkers and visitors from around the world have enjoyed rambling the slopes of Mount Tamalpais. Glorious panoramas of the Pacific coastline and San Francisco Bay were attracting walkers to the mountaintop well before Mount Tam was preserved as a state park in 1928.

If Lady Luck smiles on you, perhaps you'll experience what some Bay Area walkers call "a Farallons Day"—one of those clear days when visibility is greater than 25 miles, thus allowing a glimpse of the sharp peaks of the Farallon Islands. Germans call these clear days *Granshoen*, when the dramatic peaks of the Alps are visible from Munich. The vista from Mt. Tam is quite the granshoen.

The Mount Tamalpais and Muir Wood Railroad, known as "the crookedest railroad in the world," was constructed in 1896; it brought passengers from Mill Valley to the summit via 281 curves. Atop Mt. Tam, the Tavern of Tamalpais welcomed diners and dancers.

Redwood-lined creeks, stands of Douglas fir, and oak-dotted potreros are just a few of the great mountain's delightful environments. Thanks to the early trail building efforts of the Tamalpais Conservation Club, as well as later efforts by the CCC during the 1930s, more than 50 miles of trail explore the state park. These trails connect to two hundred more miles of trail that lead through the wooded watershed of the Marin Municipal Water District, and over to Muir Woods National Monument and Golden Gate National Recreation Area.

For many walkers, Steep Ravine Trail is a favorite mountain path; it's wet, shaded, remote. The route is along Webb Creek which, when swollen by winter rains, becomes a quite vigorous watercourse, complete with waterfalls. Redwoods, ferns, and mosses add to the feeling of walking through rain forest.

Steep Ravine Trail is, as its name suggests, a steep descent, accompanied by stair steps, and even a ladder in one place. The path intersects Dipsea Trail, which you can use to loop back to the trailhead, or follow to Stinson Beach. Many walkers descend to Stinson Beach and take the bus back up to Pantoll.

Directions to trailhead: From Highway 1, just south of Stinson Beach, turn inland on Panoramic Highway. (Note the signed Dipsea Trail, your exit

193

Steep Ravine Trail

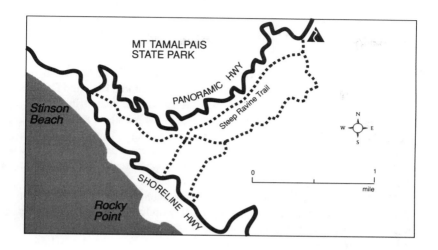

point for this walk.) Follow the highway up to Pantoll Camp and trailhead. If you're planning to take the bus from Stinson Beach back to Pantoll, remember to call the Golden Gate Transit Authority, (415) 332-6600 for schedules.

The Walk: Signed Steep Ravine Trail heads south, descending a series of switchbacks through redwood, Douglas fir and huckleberry. In a half-mile, the trail reaches Webb Creek and begins descending Steep Ravine.

Wood ferns, sword ferns, and five-finger ferns line the trail, which passes under solemn redwoods. You descend a ladder, originally built by the CCC, and cross the creek a couple of times on footbridges.

One and a half miles from the trailhead, Steep Ravine Trail is joined by Dipsea Trail, coming from the east over a footbridge. Besides retracing your steps, you have three options to consider: You may take Dipsea Trail up to Old Mine Trail, and back to Pantoll. A second alternative is to continue with Steep Ravine Trail to Highway 1, then descend to the Steep Ravine Cabins, which are available for rent, and are part of the state park. These cabins were built in the 1930s as a family retreat for Congressman William Kent, who was instrumental in preserving Mt. Tam and Muir Woods.

Most walkers choose to keep right on the Dipsea Trail and head for the town of Stinson Beach. You'll get a bird's-eye-view of the strange designs of some of the hillside homes. The trail ends close to the junction of Pamoramic Highway and Shoreline Highway. Follow the latter road to Stinson Beach—the tiny town, the sand strand, and the bus stop.

▲ 73
Coast Trail

Palomarin to Wildcat Camp: 10 1/2 miles round trip; 600-foot gain

For the homesick Brit or Scot, Pt. Reyes peninsula has more than a passing resemblance to the homeland. Inverness, Land's End, and Drake's Bay are some of the names on the land that pull on the heartstrings.

Along with its United Kingdom-like moors, weirs, glens and vales, Pt. Reyes National Seashore also has its "Lakes District." Five lakes—Bass, Pelican, Crystal, Ocean and Wildcat—were created, in part, by movement along the nearby San Andreas Fault. Earth slippage sealed off passage of spring-fed waterways, thus forming the little lakes.

The lakes are reached by a somewhat melancholy stretch of the Coast Trail, forever overhung, it seems, by dark brooding clouds. Springtime travel is a bit more cheery because the route is brightened by wildflowers: foxgloves (causing more sighs from our British friends), bush lupine, morning glory, cow parsnip and paintbrush.

Wildcat Beach, and the meadowland around Wildcat Camp, invite a picnic.

Directions to trailhead: From Stinson Beach, drive 4 1/2 miles north and take the turnoff (Olema-Bolinas Road) to Bolinas. (This turnoff is rarely signed; Bolinas residents do not have a reputation for being particularly hospitable.)

Follow this road to Mesa Road and turn right. You'll pass some brave-new-world-looking radio towers, and the Pt. Reyes Bird Observatory, and reach a large trailhead parking area at road's end.

The Walk: Coast Trail, an old farm road, ascends into a mature stand of eucalyptus, then contours out onto the cliff edge. The trail here, and in the miles to follow, is lined with coastal scrub—coyote bush, black sage, coffee berry. Turning inland, the trail descends into a gully, then climbs again back to the blufftops. Coast Trail soon repeats this maneuver, this time climbing in and out of a larger gully.

You'll pass a junction with Lake Ranch Trail, which leads, among other places, to Five Brooks Trailhead off Highway 1. A short distance beyond this junction is Bass Lake, a tranquil spot shaded by Douglas fir.

Another trail junction offers the opportunity to take Crystal Lake Trail to another lake in the "Lakes District."

Triangular-shaped Pelican Lake, perched on a blufftop, is the next lake visited by Coast Trail, which descends to another junction. A side trail leads coastward to overlook Double Point, two shale outcroppings that enclose a small bay. Seals often haul-out on the bay's small beach. Offshore stand Stormy Stacks, where California brown pelicans and cormorants roost.

Coast Trail crosses Alamere Creek, which cuts through a wild and wooded canyon on its way to the sea. During winter and spring, Alamere Falls cascading over the bluffs is an impressive sight.

A short distance beyond the creek crossing, the trail forks: the left fork, Ocean Lake Trail, and the right fork, a continuation of Coast Trail, both lead a bit over a mile to Wildcat Camp. The two trails skirt Ocean Lake and Wildcat Lake, and form a handy loop. From the camp, there's easy access to Wildcat Beach.

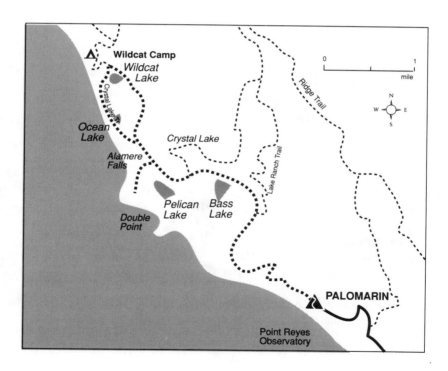

▲ 74
Bear Valley Trail

*Bear Valley Visitor Center to Divide Meadow: 3 miles round trip;
        200-foot gain*
*Bear Valley Visitor Center to Arch Rock: 8 1/2 miles round trip;
        200-foot gain*

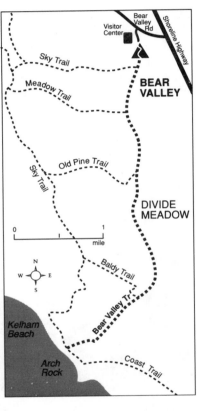

Bear Valley is the busy hub of Point Reyes National Seashore. From the park visitor center, more than 40 miles of trail lead through the valley, and to the ridges and beaches beyond. Bear Valley is a great place to begin your exploration of the 71,000-acre national seashore.

The National Park Service's Bear Valley Visitor Center is a friendly place, full of excellent history and natural history exhibits. Film screenings, a seismograph, and dioramas tell the story behind the seashore's scenery. Rangers can help you plan a walk to suit your time and inclinations.

Outside the visitor center, there is much to see, including a traditional Miwok Indian village. The family dwellings, sweat lodge, and other structures, were built using traditional Miwok methods. Near the visitor center is the Morgan Horse Ranch, where park service animals are raised and trained.

Two park interpretive trails are well worth a stroll. Woodpecker Trail is a self-guided nature trail that introduces walkers to the tremendous diversity of the region's native flora. Earthquake Trail uses old photographs and other displays to explain the seismic forces unleashed by the great 1906 San Francisco earthquake. This well-done and entertaining geology lesson is particularly relevant because most of the land west of the the San Andreas Fault Zone is within the boundaries of Pt. Reyes National Seashore.

Bear Valley Trail, a former wagon road, is surely one of the more popular paths in the national seashore. It passes through a very low gap in Inverness Ridge, and follows a nearly-level 4 1/2-mile route to the sea. First-time visitors will enjoy this easy trail. Repeat visitors will enjoy Bear Valley Trail for the access it gives to a half-dozen more remote, less-traveled trails. Some of these trails lead into the Phillip Burton Wilderness Area, which comprises about half of the national seashore. One option for the ambitious walker is the trek up 1,407-foot Mt. Wittenberg.

Directions to trailhead: Bear Valley Visitor Center at Pt. Reyes National Seashore is located just outside the town of Olema, thirty-five slow and curving miles north of San Francisco on Highway 1. A quicker route is by Highway 101, exiting on Sir Francis Drake Boulevard, traveling through the town of Fairfax and over to Olema. A left turn on Bear Valley Road takes you to the visitor center and trailhead.

The Walk: From the signed trailhead, Bear Valley Trail, an old ranch road, heads through an open meadow and passes a junction with Sky Trail, which ascends Mt. Wittenberg. Beyond this junction, the trail enters a forest of Bishop pine and Douglas fir. Your path is alongside Bear Valley Creek.

Notice that the creek flows north, in the opposite direction of Coast Creek, which you'll soon be following from Divide Meadow to the sea. This strange drainage pattern is one more example of how the mighty San Andreas Fault can shape the land.

A half-mile along, you'll pass a second side trail, Meadow Trail, and after another mile of travel, arrive at Divide Meadow. A hunt club, visited by Presidents William Howard Taft and Theodore Roosevelt, once stood here. During the early part of this century, meadows and nearby forested ridges abounded with deer, bear, mountain lion, and game birds.

Well-named Divide Meadow divides Bear Valley Creek from Coast Creek, which you'll soon be following when you continue on Bear Valley Trail. Divide Meadow is a fine place to picnic.

Shady Bear Valley Trail junctions with a couple more trails, including Glen Camp Trail which leads to one of the national seashore's backpacker camps. Near the ocean, Bear Valley Trail emerges from the forest and arrives at an open meadow on the precipitous bluffs above Arch Rock. At low tide, you can squeeze through a sea tunnel at the mouth of Coast Creek.

Unpack your lunch, unfold your map, and plan a return route by way of one of Bear Valley's many scenic trails.

▲ 75
Estero Trail

Estero Trailhead to Drake's Estero: 8 miles round trip; 500-foot gain

This coast walk will keep you glued to your field glasses. No, the route isn't difficult to follow; you'll want the field glasses to help you observe the abundant wildlife around Drake's Estero. The many fingers of Drake's Estero, Marin County's largest lagoon, is patrolled by canvas backs, ruddy ducks and American widgeons. Great blue herons, willets, godwits and many, many more shorebirds feed along the mudflats. You might see deer, either the native black- tail or the "imported" white axis browsing the grassy ridges. Harbor seals and sea lions often swim into the estero.

You won't need binoculars to sight the most common animal found in these parts—cows. Both Herefords and Black Angus graze the headlands. This is cow country, and has been for over a hundred years. A century ago, schooners maneuvered into Drake's Estero, took on cargo of fine butter, and returned to San Francisco, a ready market for the dairy products produced on Point Reyes.

The estero you'll visit, as well as the beach and bay you'll overlook, are named for that pirate/explorer in the service of Queen Elizabeth I, Sir Francis Drake. While you're walking along the estero, you can debate that age-old question: Did Sir Francis in June of 1579 sail his Golden Hinde into Drake's Bay or into San Francisco Bay? Is he the discoverer of San Francisco Bay, or does that honor fall to other sailors, more than two hundred years later?

The bay where Drake set anchor had chalky cliffs, and reminded the Englishman of the cliffs of Dover. Drake's description of this bay points to Drake's Bay. To mark his discovery, Drake left a brass plate nailed to a post. This plate was found in 1936 and authenticated as being Drake's; however the man who unearthed the plate claimed to have found it near San Quentin Prison on San Francisco Bay. And so the debate goes on...

Old ranch roads form a nice trail system on the west side of Inverness Ridge. Estero Trail is the most dramatic of these trails, and offers fine vistas and superb wildlife-viewing opportunities.

Directions to trailhead: From Highway 1 in Olema (where there's a well-marked turnoff for the Point Reyes National Seashore Bear Valley Visitor Center), proceed two miles north and veer left onto Sir Francis Drake Highway. The highway follows the west side of Tomales Bay, passes through the hamlet of Inverness, then heads left (west). You'll pass a junction on your left with a road leading toward Mt. Vision. Keep looking left and you'll see the signed road leading to Estero parking area. Follow this narrow road to the signed trailhead.

The Walk: Estero Trail, an old ranch road, climbs gently. As you climb, look over your left shoulder and admire Inverness Ridge, highlighted by, from west to east, Mt. Vision, Pt. Reyes Hill, and Mt. Wittenberg.

The trail turns to the left, and passes a stand of pine, once the nucleus of a Christmas Tree farm. Soon the path crosses a causeway, which divides Home Bay from a pond. Bird watchers will sight large numbers of shorebirds in the mudflats of Home Bay.

The trail rises above the estero, descends to another pond, and ascends again. About 2 1/2 miles from the trailhead, you come to a signed junction. Sunset Beach Trail continues well above the estero, and ends at a couple of small ponds, backed by Drake's Bay and the wide Pacific.

Estero Trail swings east and after a half mile comes to a junction. You may head south on Drake's Head Trail down to Limantour Estero, or you may follow Estero Trail all the way to Limantour Beach.

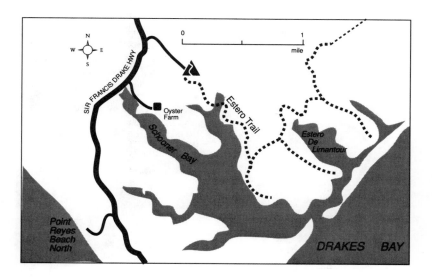

▲ 76
Johnstone Trail

Heart's Desire Beach to Jepson Memorial Grove:
3 miles round trip; 300-foot gain
Heart's Desire Beach to Shell Beach: 8 miles round trip; 300-foot gain

Two lovely trails, named for a professor and a planner, explore Tomales Bay State Park. Botanist Willis Jepson, founder of the School of Forestry at the University of California, Berkeley, and author of the authoritative "Manual of the Flowering Plants of California," is honored by the Jepson Trail.

Conservationist Bruce Johnstone, Marin County planner, and his wife Elsie, worked long and hard to preserve Tomales Bay and place part of it in a state park. Johnstone Trail leads bayside from Pebble Beach to Shell Beach.

Bay area walkers have a little secret: When fog smothers Pt. Reyes and San Francisco Bay, try heading for Tomales Bay State Park. The park has a microclimate, and often has sunny days and pleasant temperatures when other neighboring coastal locales are damp and cold.

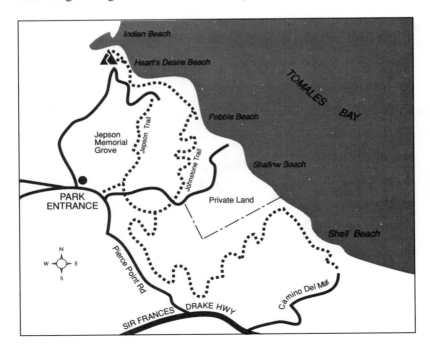

Directions to trailhead: Your goal is Tomales Bay State Park, located on the east side of Pt. Reyes Peninsula. From the town of Inverness, follow Sir Francis Drake Boulevard to Pierce Point Road. Turn right and drive a half-mile to the entrance to Tomales Bay State Park. Follow signs to the large parking lot at Heart's Desire Beach.

The Walk: Near the trailhead are some interpretive displays that tell of clams (Can you dig them?), and Bishop pine. Signed Johnstone Trail departs from the south end of Heart's Desire Beach and immediately climbs into a lush, moss-draped forest of oak, bay, madrone, and wax myrtle.

A half-mile of travel brings you to a picnic area on the bluffs above Pebble Beach. At a trail junction, a short side trail goes straight down to Pebble Beach, but Johnstone Trail swings southwest and begins switchbacking up forested slopes. Some wetter areas of the coastal slope are dotted with ferns. The trail crosses a paved road and soon junctions. If you want to continue to Shell Beach, you'll bear left with the Johnstone Trail. In 1980, California's young adult conservation corps extended the Johnstone Trail to Shell Beach. The trail detours around some private property, and contours over the coastal slope at an elevation of about 500 feet. The path leads through Bishop pine and a lush understory of salal and huckleberry bushes. After a few miles, the trail descends through madrone and oak forest to Shell Beach.

Walkers content with looping back to Heart's Desire Beach via Jepson Trail will continue straight at the above- mentioned junction. Bishop pine, along with its similar-looking piney cousins, the Monterey and knobcone, are known as fire pines, because they require the heat of fire to crack open their cones and release their seeds. Bishop pines are slow to propagate and are relatively rare in coastal California. (Another nice stand of Bishop pine is located in Montana de Oro State Park in San Luis Obispo County.)

The surest way to distinguish a Bishop pine from its look-alike, the Monterey pine, is by counting the needles: Monterey pines have three needles to a bunch, Bishop pines have two needles to a cluster.

Some strategically-placed benches allow walkers to savor the fine bay views afforded by the Jepson Trail, which descends gently to Heart's Desire Beach.

Bishop pine cone

▲ 77
Tomales Point Trail

Upper Pierce Ranch to Lower Pierce Ranch:
6 miles round trip; 300-foot gain
Upper Pierce Ranch to Tomales Point: 8 miles round trip; 400-foot gain

When the fog settles over the dew-dampened grasslands of Tomales Point, walkers can easily imagine that they're stepping onto a Scottish moor, or wandering one of the Shetland Islands.

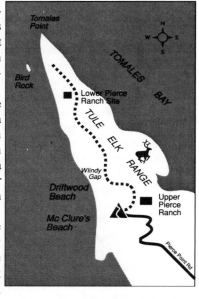

The point's rich pasture caught the eye of Solomon Pierce, who began a dairy in 1858. Pierce and his son Abram produced fine butter, which was shipped to San Francisco from a wharf they built on Tomales Bay. For seven decades, the point remained in the Pierce family.

The walk begins at Upper Pierce Ranch, where the Pierce family house, barn, and outbuildings are now maintained by the National Park Service. The path, the old ranch road, wanders over the green hills, which are seasonally sprinkled with yellow poppies and tidy tips, orange fiddleneck, and purple iris. A small pond and an eucalyptus grove mark the site of Lower Pierce Ranch.

Dramatic views of the Point Reyes area are available from Tomales Point, the northernmost boundary of Marin County and Point Reyes National Seashore.

Directions to trailhead: Drive north on Sir Francis Drake Boulevard past the town of Inverness. Shortly after Sir Francis turns west, bear right (north) on Pierce Point Road, and follow this road nine miles to its end at Upper Pierce Point Ranch. Tomales Point Trail shares a trailhead with the half-mile long path leading to McClures Beach.

The Walk: From the old dairy buildings at Upper Pierce Ranch, the trail climbs north across the coastal prairie. Views of the beach and surf are superb. Be on the lookout for the Tule elk herd that wanders the bluffs. A large elk population once roamed the Point Reyes area, but by the 1860s, hunters had eliminated the animals. In 1977, the National Park Service relocated some elk onto Tomales Point from the Owens Valley.

The wide path climbs and descends at a moderate rate. As you crest the ridge and meander over to its eastern side, you'll begin to get a view of Tomales Bay, as well as Hog Island and the village of Dillon Beach. The old ranch road descends to the site of Lower Pierce Ranch, and you'll pass a pond and an eucalyptus grove.

Soon the road becomes a trail, and a mile past the ranch, arrives at a high vista point that looks down on Bird Rock. The rock is occupied by cormorants, and by white pelicans.

A faint path, and some cross-country travel, will take you to the very top of Tomales Point for stirring views of Bodega Head and Tomales Bay.

Tule elk roam Tomales Point

▲ 78
Bodega Head Trail

Bodega Head to Horseshoe Cove Overlook: 1 mile round trip
Bodega Head to Salmon Creek Beach: 4 1/2 miles round trip

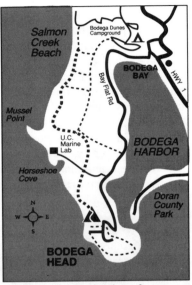

Anchoring the south end of the Sonoma Coast State Beaches is the massive granite monolith of Bodega Rock. The great rock lies just west of the San Andreas Fault. Geologists speculate that the inexorable creep of the Pacific Plate along the fault carried the rock to this location from the Tehachapi Mountains, more than 300 miles away to the southeast.

Bodega Head's beauty is marred only by a huge hole dug on its harbor side. The hole in the head, as it's known, is a reminder that Bodega Bay was slated to become the site of one of the largest nuclear power plants in America. When in the early 1960s conservationists protested the desecration of the landscape, and geologists raised seismic saftety questions, construction of the nuclear plant was halted. The hole in the head is now undergoing environmental rehabilitation.

This walk, from the tip of Bodega Head up the peninsula to Salmon Creek, is a delight. You'll have an opportunity to explore the Bodega Dunes, some of the tallest in the state. And you can walk two-mile long Salmon Creek Beach, longest sand strand in Sonoma County.

Directions to trailhead: From Highway 1 in the town of Bodega Bay, turn west on Bay Flat Road. Follow this road, which veers south, and becomes known as Westside Road. The road forks. The left fork leads to a parking area overlooking the bay side of Bodega Head. Take the right fork to road's end at the signed Bodega Head Trail.

The Walk: From the Bodega Head trailhead, the path climbs north. You'll soon get good views of Bodega Head, and of fishing boats passing through the narrow entrance to Bodega Harbor.

A half-mile of travel brings you to a signed junction. The right fork is the main trail leading to the dunes and beach, but take the left fork 1/10 of a mile so that you can enjoy the terrific vistas from Horseshoe Cove Overlook.

The southern view takes in Bodega Bay, and quite a bit of Marin County coastline, including the northern point of Point Reyes National Seashore. To the north, you'll glimpse Horseshoe Cove, Salmon Creek Beach, and a number of the pocket beaches and coves within the Sonoma Coast State Beaches. The building you see is the University of California's Bodega Marine Laboratory, a research and teaching facility. Part of the Bodega peninsula's ocean-facing coastline and a stretch of bay shore is protected by Bodega Marine Reserve. This reserve, along with a number of others around the state, are part of the University of California's Natural Reserve System that help protect fragile environments and promote research.

From back at the trail junction, Bodega Head Trail leads north up and over a low rise. Coyote bush and other coastal scrub vegetation line the trail. A sign informs you that you've entered the U.C. Reserve and to "Enjoy your Hike and Please Stay on the Trail." The path soon crosses the road leading to the marine lab and enters the dunes. Wooden posts help you stay on the sandy trail, which is bit confusing in places.

Once brome grass and rye grass covered the dunes, but these native grasses were grazed—in fact, overgrazed—by livestock. The dunes, naturally unstable and subject to the whims of the wind, were fast blowing away when in 1951, European beach grass was planted. This grass, used to protect dikes in the Netherlands, has helped control the drifting sand, and kept it from blowing into the bay.

After climbing the dunes, you'll exit the reserve, and descend to a signed junction. A sharp right would take you up and over a hill to Westside County Park on Bodega Bay. Heading straight ahead, north, will put you on the Riding and Hiking Loop, a trail popular with equestrians, that loops around the dunes and leads 1 1/2 miles to Bodega Dunes Campground.

Continue on Bodega Head Trail, which veers west 1/2 mile to driftwood-strewn Salmon Creek Beach. You can beachcomb north two miles along Salmon Creek Beach, which is fringed with beach strawberry and sand verbena. You can also walk the same distance on the parallel horse path that crosses the dunes above the beach.

79

Sonoma Coast Trail

Blind Beach to Shell Beach: 4 miles round trip
Blind Beach to Wright's Beach: 6 1/2 miles round trip

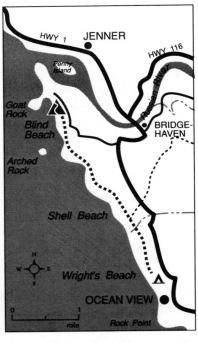

The names alone are intriguing: Blind Beach and Schoolhouse Beach, Arched Rock and Goat Rock, Penny Island and Bodega Head. These colorfully-named locales are some of the highlights of Sonoma Coast State Beach, thirteen miles of coastline stretching from the Russian River to Bodega Bay.

Sonoma Coast State Beach is not one beach, but many. You could easily overlook them, because most aren't visible from Highway 1. The beaches are tucked away in rocky coves, and hidden by tall bluffs.

Sonoma Coast Trail is a pretty, blufftop route that connects some of these secret beaches. It crosses pastureland grazed by sheep. During spring, wildflowers brighten the bluff: blue lupine, Indian paintbrush, western wallflower, and sea fig.

Sonoma Coast Trail begins on the bluffs above Blind Beach, but the walker can also begin at Goat Rock, located a half-mile north of the trailhead. The rock is connected to the mainland by a causeway. During the 1920s, Goat Rock was quarried, and used to build a jetty at the mouth of the Russian River.

A mile north of the trailhead, and a half-mile north of Goat Rock is the mouth of the Russian River. The 110-mile long river is one of the largest on the north coast. At the river mouth, you can observe ospreys nesting in the treetops. The California brown pelican is one of several species of birds that feed and nest on Penny Island, located in the river mouth.

Directions to trailhead: From Highway 1, ten miles north of the town of Bodega Bay, turn west on Goat Rock Road. Signed Sonoma CoastTrail begins at a small parking lot on the left of the road. If you'd like to begin this walk at Goat Rock, continue to road's end at a large parking area.

The Walk: Sonoma Coast Trail heads south along the edge of the bluffs. Soon, you'll step over a stile and head across a pasture. The trail climbs to a saddle on the shoulder of Peaked Hill (elevation 376 feet).

You then descend to the flat, grassy blufftops, and cross a bridge over a fern-lined ravine. It's a pastoral scene: Sheep graze the bluffs, and in the distance stands a weathered old barn.

After crossing another ravine, the path reaches the Shell Beach parking area. A short trail descends the bluffs to Shell Beach. Another trail extends northwest, crosses the highway, and reaches redwood-shaded Willow Creek. Picnic tables and walk-in (environmental) campsites are located near the creek.

Sonoma Coast Trail continues south, detouring inland around a private home, then doubling back seaward. The trail plunges into Furlong Gulch, then switchbacks back up to the bluffs. You can may follow the trail, or the beach, to Wright's Beach Campground.

Sonoma Coast State Beach

80

Fort Ross Trail

Fort Ross to Fort Ross Cove: 1/2 mile round trip
Fort Ross to Reef Point Campground: 4 miles round trip

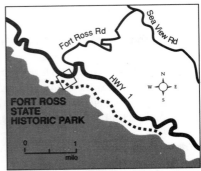

Fort Ross, the last remnant of Czarist Russia's foothold in California, is today a walker's delight. Near the fort, sinuous Highway 1 suddenly straightens. You look out upon a handsome, windswept bluff, and spy a redwood stockade and Russian Orthodox Chapel. For the first-time visitor, it's a startling sight.

Napoleon was beginning his 1812 invasion of Russia when Fort Ross—named for Rossiya, itself—was built. The fort's location ideally suited the purposes of the colony. The site was easily defensible. Tall trees, necessary for the fort's construction and the shipbuilding that would take place in the nearby cove, covered the coastal slopes. The waters were full of sea otters—an attraction for the Russian American Fur Company, which would soon hunt the animals to near-extinction. Wheat, potatoes, and vegetables were grown on the coastal terrace, and shipped to Russian settlements in Alaska. All in all, the fort was nearly self-sufficient.

Thanks to the state's replication and restoration efforts, the fort's buildings bring back the flavor of the Russians' foray into North America. The high stockade, built entirely of hand-hewn redwood timber, looks particularly formidable.

Also of interest is the seven-sided blockhouse, with its interpretive exhibits, and the small, wooden, Orthodox Chapel. And be sure to stop at the Fort Ross Visitors Center, a new facility with Russian, Pomo Indian, and natural history exhibits.

When you've completed your walk through history, another surprise awaits: a walk out on the lonely, beautiful headlands.

Directions to trailhead: Fort Ross State Historic Park is located off of Highway 1, some 12 miles north of the village of Jenner by the Sea.

Restored Russian-Orthodox chapel, Fort Ross

The Walk: Exit the fort's main gate, follow the stockade walls to the left, and join the downhill path. It's a short walk to secluded Fort Ross Cove, one of California's first shipyards. You'll find an interpretive display and picnic tables here.

Cross Fort Ross Creek on a small footbridge. The mighty San Andreas Fault has altered the course of the creek by more than a half mile. Follow the path inland along the creek, which is lined with bay laurel, willow, and alder. After a few hundred yards of travel, look to your right for an unmarked, narrow path leading south.

The indistinct path travels onto an open coastal terrace. You'll no doubt see some sheep eating the pastoral vegetation. Follow the undulations of the rye grass and barley covered headland, and meander first southeast, then southwest. Continue south until you spot a path leading down to a dirt road. (Don't try to climb the sheep fence; use the stile located where the road deadends.)

Descend the dirt road to Reef Campground, formerly a private campground, and now a state park facility. It's a good place for a picnic.

Across the road, another stile beckons to the entrance of Sonoma County's "Lost Coast," so named because high cliffs and high tides keep this seven miles of beach elusive to most walkers.

A mile of walking across boulder-strewn beaches brings you to Fort Ross Reef, which discourages further progress.

211

81

Kruse Rhododendron Loop Trail

2 1/4 miles round trip; 200-foot gain

One of the annual rites, and fine sights, of spring is a walk amongst the pale pink blossoms of Kruse Rhododendron State Reserve. The California rhododendrons festoon the forest floor from about mid-April to mid-June.

The rhododendron's success depends on its struggle for light in a dark world, dominated by the tanbark oak, Douglas fir, and redwood. A severe forest fire that scorched the slopes of Kruse Ranch was reponsible for the sudden emergence of the rhododendrons here. Now, as the tall tree forest regenerates, it restricts the light available to the rhododendrons, thereby diminishing their grand display.

The Kruse family established a ranch here in 1880, raised sheep, and extensively logged the coastal slopes. Edward Kruse donated the land to the state in 1933, in memory of his father, who was the founder of San Francisco's German Bank—later, First Western Bank.

Directions to trailhead: Kruse Rhododendron State Reserve adjoins Salt Point State Park. Turn east off Highway 1 onto steep Kruse Ranch Road and travel 1/2 mile to the trailhead.

The Walk: Since this is a loop trail, you may begin from the leg north of Kruse Ranch Road or from the leg to the south.

The trail crosses two gulches—Chinese and Phillips. You'll explore the mouths of these gulches if you take the Salt Point Trail through the state park.

Those walkers wishing to stretch their legs a bit, may leave the loop trail a mile from the trailhead, where the path crosses Kruse Ranch Road. It's possible to follow this dirt road for a mile to Stump Beach Trail, then follow this latter path 1 1/4 mile back to Highway 1, where it rounds Stump Beach Cove.

Trails 81 & 82

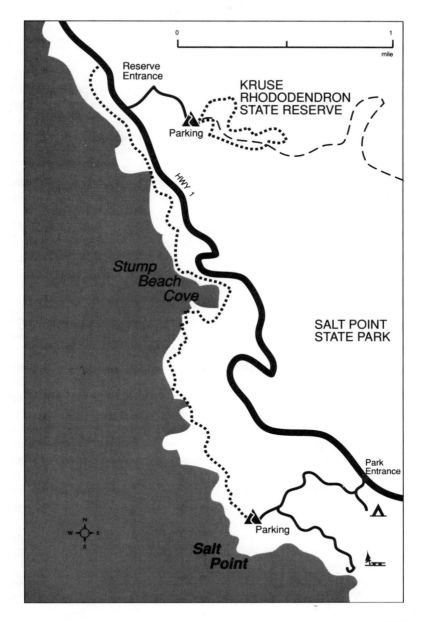

Reserve
Entrance

KRUSE
RHODODENDRON
STATE RESERVE

Parking

HWY 1

Stump
Beach
Cove

SALT POINT
STATE PARK

Park
Entrance

Parking

Salt
Point

N
W   E
S

213

▲ 82
Salt Point Trail

Salt Point to Stump Beach Cove: 2 1/2 miles round trip
Salt Point to Fisk Mill Cove: 6 miles round trip

Sheer, sandstone cliffs, and sandy coves highlight Salt Point State Park's seven miles of coastline. Tidepools, sea stacks, and sea caves add to the drama of a blufftop walk.

Marine life is abundant in the tidepools. One of the first underwater reserves to be set aside in California—Gerstle Cove—is popular with divers.

Several midden sites found within park boundaries suggest that Pomo and Coast Yuki Indians spent many summers camped on this coast. The Indians gathered abalone, and salt to preserve seafood.

Directions to trailhead: Salt Point State Park is located about seven miles north of Fort Ross; eighteen miles north of Jenner. From Highway 1, turn west into the park's campground and follow signs to Marine Terrace Parking Area.

The Walk: Head north atop the dramatic bluffs of Salt Point. In a quarter-mile, you'll cross Warren Creek. At the creek mouth is a little cove, one of about a dozen you'll encounter along the state park's coastline.

The coves are quiet now, but in the last century there was much activity. Aleut hunters, brought to nearby Fort Ross by the Russian American Fur Company, hunted otters and seals. Lumber schooners maneuvered into the coves to load redwoods logged from nearby slopes.

The path reaches the bluffs above Stump Beach Cove, which is not, as you might suspect, named for the remains of redwoods logged nearby; instead, the name honors Sheriff Stump, law and order for Salt Point township.

An old farm road leads down to the cove, where there's a picnic area. You can sit a while, and watch the terns, cormorants, gulls, osprey, and brown pelicans.

To continue this walk, you follow a newly-constructed trail up the north slope above Stump Creek. Rejoining the bluffs, you dip in and out of Phillips Gulch, Chinese Gulch, and other little gullies.

The path is not particularly distinct, and you must devise your own route along the edge of the grassy headlands. Photographers will marvel at the spectacle of surf meeting rock. Waterfalls spill into the picturesque coves

Divers scout waters of Gerstle Cove, Salt Point State Park

at the mouths of Chinese and Phillips Gulches.

The trail becomes easier to follow, and alternates between open meadowland and wind-sculpted stands of Bishop pine and Douglas fir.

A good destination is the picnic area south of Fisk Mill Cove. Or you can even continue another two miles north to Horseshoe Cove at the northern end of the state park. (See page 213 for map.)

▲ 83
Gualala Point Trail

Visitors Center to Gualala River mouth: 1 1/2 miles round trip
Visitors Center to Sea Ranch, Return via Blufftop Trail, Salal Trail:
4 1/2 miles round trip

Gualala, the name of a river, a point, a town and a park located on the northern boundary of Sonoma County offers some fascinating walks. Hurried travelers can exit Highway 1 and stretch their legs with a short walk along Gualala River. Walkers with more time will enjoy exploring all the environments of Gualala Point Regional Park— ocean, river and forest. Environmental activists and those who have been observing the two-decade-long struggle to open Sea Ranch to public use, will relish the chance to explore this newly-accessible stretch of coastline.

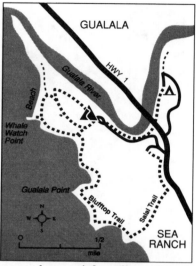

The origin of the name Gualala has never been satisfactorily explained. Anthropologists suggest that is the Spanish rendering of the Pomo Indian word walali—"where the waters meet." Some historians speculate that Ernest Rufus, a captain in John Sutter's Indian Company and the 1846 grantee of Rancho German, gave the area its name. Walhalla in Teutonic mythology is the abode of heroes fallen in battle.

Unlike most California coastal rivers and creeks, which cascade westerly from the slopes of the coastal mountains, the Gualala flows south to north— along the San Andreas Fault. A sandspit forms at the river mouth in summer, when this area can best be explored on foot. Near the Coast Highway bridge is a freshwater marsh, habitat for water and shore birds. A redwood grove, accompanied by rhododendrons and sword ferns, lines an upper stretch of the river. These diverse Gualala River habitats can be explored via the highly recommended 3/4-mile-long River Trail.

Be sure to check out the exhibits in the park's visitors center. A wind generator system provides power for the building. It's one of the first uses of wind generation to power a public building.

Directions to trailhead: Gualala Point Regional Park is located off Highway 1, a half-mile south of the town of Gualala. (The first left inside the park leads to the trailhead for Salal Trail which you'll pass if you decide to pursue the Sea Ranch option of this walk.) Continue a half-mile through the park to the visitors center.

The Walk: From the visitors center, follow the paved path for a hundred yards. Join a grassy trail and descend to the river mouth.

After exploring the river mouth, double back to a line of cypress trees and head south on the blufftop trail to Whale Watch Point. At a fence line delineating the park boundary, you can either loop back to the trailhead or walk through the fence into Sea Ranch on the blufftop trail.

The trail into Sea Ranch plunges into a stand of cypress. When you emerge you'll spy the golf course, dotted with deer and golfers. State Coastal Conservancy trail signs keep you on the track, which doggedly follows the bluffs.

Near the path are several Bauhaus-inspired homes, done in an architectural style sometimes described as "grain elevator modern." Some architects believe that this severe style blends in with the surroundings; others have their doubts.

You round cypress-covered Gualala Point and cross a wooden footbridge. After walking across a grassy headland you reach a junction with Salal Trail on the bluffs above a rocky pocket beach.

Salal Trail crosses a paved path and joins the creekbed. (On brisk days, it's a refuge from the wind.) The path winds past a stand of redwood and through dense berry bushes. Crossing a small bridge and a paved road, the trail continues with Salal Creek through a densely vegetated area of ferns, Bishop pine and cypress. You emerge from Salal Creek drainage near Highway 1. Head north on the path paralleling the highway.

A quarter-mile of travel brings you to the Salal trailhead and the Gualala Point Regional Park day use area. From here, it's a half-mile jaunt along the road back to the park visitors center.

84

Fern Canyon Trail

Van Damme State Park Campground to Fern Canyon:
5 miles round trip; 200-foot gain
Campground to Pygmy Forest: 7 miles round trip; 400-foot gain

Five-finger and bird's foot, lady and licorice, stamp, sword and deer—
these are some of the colorful names of the ferns growing in well-named Fern
Canyon. This lush canyon, the heart of Van Damme State Park, is also rich
with young redwoods, red alder, big leaf maple and Douglas fir, as well as
a tangled understory of Oregon grape and berry bushes.

Little River meanders through Fern Canyon, as does a lovely trail which
crosses the river nine times. Fern Canyon Trail, paved along its lower
stretch, follows the route of an old logging skid road. For three decades,
beginning in 1864, ox teams hauled timber through the canyon.

A lumber mill once stood at the mouth of Little River. During the late
nineteenth century, schooners used for shipping logs and lumber were
constructed at a boatworks located at the river mouth. Lumberman, boat
builder, San Francisco businessman Charles F. Van Damme was born in the
hamlet of Little River. He purchased land on the site of the former sawmill
and bequeathed the river mouth and canyon to the state park system.

In Van Damme State Park, another very special environment awaits the
walker: the Pygmy Forest. A nutrient-poor, highly acidic topsoil, combined
with a dense hardpan located beneath the surface that resists root penetra-
tion, has severely restricted the growth of trees in certrain areas of the coastal
shelf between Salt Point and Fort Bragg. The Pygmy Forest in Van Damme
State Park is truly Lilliputian. Sixty-year-old cypress trees are but a few feet
tall and measure a half inch in diameter.

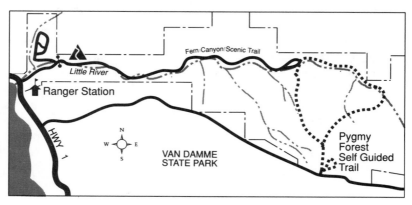

Fern Canyon, Van Damme State Park

The walker has a choice of two trails that lead to the Pygmy Forest. One route loops 3 1/2 miles through Fern Canyon; another, the one-mile long Logging Road Trail leads more directly to the forest. A self-guided nature trail, built upon an elevated wooden walkway, loops through the Pygmy Forest.

Directions to trailhead: Van Damme State Park is located off Highway 1, three miles south of Mendocino. Turn inland on the main park road, and follow it through the canyon to a parking area at the beginning of signed Fern Canyon Trail.

The Walk: The first and second crossings of Little River will give you an inkling of what lies ahead. During summer, the river is easily forded; in winter, expect to get your feet wet.

The wide path brings you close to elderberry, salmonberry and a multitude of ferns. Two miles and eight river crossings later, you'll pass the state park's environmental campsites—reserved for walkers and bicyclists.

The road splits into a short loop and the two forks rejoin at the end of the paved road. Both trails lead to Pygmy Forest. To the left, the longer loop continues east through Fern Canyon before joining the old logging road and traveling to Pygmy Forest. For a shorter walk to Pygmy Forest, cross Little River and follow the Old Logging Road Trail a mile.

▲ 85
Mendocino Headlands Trail

Mendocino to Big River Beach: 2 miles round trip
Mendocino to state park boundary: 2 miles round trip

Few coastal locales are as photographed·as the town of Mendocino and its bold headlands. The town itself, which lies just north of the mouth of Big River, resembles a New England village, no doubt by design of its Yankee founders. Now protected by a state park, the headlands are laced with paths that offer postcard views of wave tunnels and tidepools, beaches and blowholes.

Like the town, the headlands have a storied past. Booldam—"Big River"—is what Pomo Indians called the village here. Wave tunnels, one measuring more than 700 feet long, penetrate the Mendocino Bay bluffs; they've been the death of many ships—particularly during the days of sail, when a number of vessels were reportedly blown into these tunnels and never seen again.

Despite rough surf conditions, one of California's first doghole ports was located here. A railway, built in 1853, carried redwood lumber from a nearby mill to a chute located on the point. It was a tricky loading operation, to say the least.

Once the most cosmopolitan of little ports, Mendocino declined in economic and cultural importance as the logging industry came to a halt in the 1930s. The town revived in the 1950s when a number of San Francisco artists established the Mendocino Art Center. What was bohemian and cheap in the 1950s is now upscale and pricey, but the town's Maine village-look has been preserved. Mendocino's citizenry not only preserved the town in a historical district, but succeeded in placing the majestic bluffs, threatened with a modern subdivision, under the protection of Mendocino Headlands State Park in 1972. Mendocino is a great town for the walker to explore. Grand Victorian houses and simple New England salt boxes mingle with a downtown that includes several fascinating nineteenth-century buildings. Among the architectural gems are the Masonic Hall, built in 1866 and topped with a redwood sculpture of Father Time, the Medocino Hotel with its antique decor and the Presbyterian Church, constructed in 1867 and now a state historical landmark.

A summer walk onto the headlands allows you to escape the crowds, while a winter walk, perhaps when a storm is brewing offshore, is a special experience indeed. From the end of town you can walk down-coast to Big River or up-coast to a blowhole.

Directions to trailhead: From "downtown" Mendocino, follow Main Street up coast past the Mendocino Hotel to Heeser Street. Park wherever you can find a space. The unsigned trail leads southwest through a fence. The trail soon forks; the route down-coast to Big River Beach is described first.

The Walk: Heading east, the trail soon brings you to some blufftop benches and a coastal accessway leading down to Portagee Beach.

Wooden steps cross a gully and the trail soon forks— offering both a route along the edge of the bluffs and another heading on a straighter course toward Big River.

Notice the crossties, remains of the old oxen-powered railway that hauled lumber to the bluff edge, where it was then sent by chute to waiting ships.

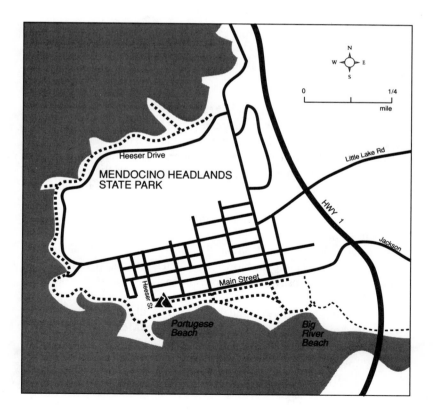

From the bluff edge, lumber was sent by
chute to waiting ships

Wildflowers seasonally brightening the grassy headlands include
lupine and Mendocino Coast paintbrush. More noticeable are non-
native species, domestic flowers
gone wild—nasturtiums, calla lilies, hedge rose—as well as Scotch broom,
an unwelcome pest that thrives in many North Coast state parks.

After meandering past some Bishop pine, the path descends moderately
to steeply to the beach where Big River empties into Mendocino Bay. The
quarter-mile long beach is part of Mendocino Headlands State Park. Back
of the beach is a marsh, Big River Estuary, a winter stopover for ducks and
geese. Salmon and steelhead spawn up river.

Return the same way or detour through town to admire some of
Mendocino's historical buildings.

Option: To Blowhole and beyond. Bearing right at the first trail junction
from the trailhead, leads to the blowhole, which is encircled by a low fence.
While no aqueous Vesuvius, the blowhole can at times be a frothy and
picturesque cauldron.

The path continues north along the edge of headlands for another mile.
You'll pass a plaque dedicated by the sister cities of Mendocino and Miasa,
Japan "to the peaceful pursuit of the peoples of the Pacific basin and to the
protection of its environment that all living things therein may exist in
perpetual harmony."

Quaint Mendocino town resembles a New England fishing village, circa 1907

86

Russian Gulch Trail

Campground to Falls: 6 1/2 miles round trip; 200-foot gain

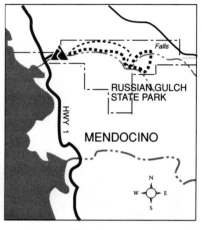

Russian Gulch is a lush coastal range canyon filled with second generation redwoods, Douglas fir and California laurel. Beneath the tall trees grows a lush understory of ferns, berry bushes, azaleas and rhododendrons.

Gulch and state park take their name from the Fort Ross-based Russian fur hunters who trapped in this area during the first quarter of the nineteenth century. Historians speculate that the gulch was one of the places where the hunters cached otter skins.

Russian Gulch offers walkers the chance to experience several distinct biotic communities. The mouth of the canyon is framed, as if in a photograph, by a handsome Coast Highway bridge. A beach offers swimming and sunning; however, the cold waters here are more popular as an entry point for wetsuit-clad divers. Urchins and abalone populate the rich subtidal area.

Above the river mouth, the park headlands offer great north and south coastal views, as well as glimpses of Russian Gulch itself. Out on the headlands, seasonally bedecked with Douglas iris and poppies, is the Devil's Punchbowl, a wave tunnel that's collapsed to form a 100-foot- diameter hole. This blowhole, while too large to blow very much, is nevertheless an inspiring sight when the surf wells up inside the hole.

The trail system through Russian Gulch State Park offers a number of alternatives. You may take a direct or a more roundabout route through the canyon and either a longer or shorter route to the waterfall. It's possible to combine all trail options into a delightful nine-mile tour of the park.

Directions to trailhead: Russian Gulch State Park is located two miles north of the town of Mendocino. The trail, a continuation of the park road that's been closed to vehicle traffic, departs from the east end of the campground.

The Walk: The paved trail, suitable for bicycles, is nearly flat for the first mile as it winds along with the stream. Along the bottom of the gulch grow alder, willow and big leaf maple. On higher canyon slopes are western hemlock and second-growth redwoods. The forest was even thicker before early loggers cleared the canyon.

Two miles of travel brings you to a small picnic area, where you'll find a couple of picnic tables beneath the redwoods. A short distance past the picnic area, you'll spot signed North Trail, which leads northwest back to the park campground; consider this path as an alternate return route. Continue about 100 feet past this trail junction to the signed beginning of the waterfall loop.

Russian Gulch forks here and so does the trail. Take the left, shorter, route and climb by trail, wooden steps and footbridges 3/4 mile to the falls. The falls cascade 36 feet into a small grotto.

If you continue on the loop trail (this adds one more mile to your walk), you'll climb stone steps above the falls, then switchback away from the creek through tanoak forest. After topping a ridge, the trail drops into the south fork of Russian Gulch and returns you to the lower trail junction and the return route to the trailhead.

Highway One Bridge, Russian Gulch

▲ 87
Jug Handle Ecological Staircase Trail

5 miles round trip; 300-foot gain

The watershed of Jug Handle Creek holds a rare natural phenomenon—an "ecological staircase"—that attracts scientists and nature lovers from all over the world. The staircase is composed of five terraces, each 100,000 years older, and 100 feet higher than the one below it.

The terraces were sculpted into the sandstone cliffs by wave action. As a result of tectonic action—our North American plate crunching against the offshore Pacific plate—the terraces were uplifted. In fact, today the terraces continue their inexorable uplift at the rate of an inch per century. Wave action is ever-so-slowly forming a sixth terrace at the mouth of Jug Handle Creek.

Terraces, and the forces forming them, are by no means unique to Jug Handle Creek; however, in most California coastal locales, the terraces are eroded and indistinct. Only at the state reserve are the evolutionary sequences so distinguishable, and so well preserved.

Your walk up the staircase will be greatly aided if you pick up an interpretive pamphlet from the little park headquarters building or from the vending machine out front. However, even without a natural history lesson, this is a pleasant and absorbing walk.

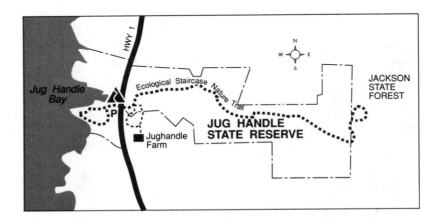

Directions to trailhead: Five miles south of Fort Bragg, and just south of Jug Handle Creek bridge, turn west off Highway 1 into the Jug Handle Reserve parking area.

The Walk: Head west on the signed trail out onto the grassy blufftops. The trail loops toward the edge of the bluffs, offers a view of Jug Handle Cove, then returns east to dip under the highway bridge.

The first terrace supports native grassland, and wind-sculpted Sitka spruce.

Second-growth redwood trees are the most noticeable feature of the second terrace.

The upper terraces are the site of the Mendocino Pygmy Forest. Cypress and pine are but five to ten feet tall, and shrubs such as rhododendron, manzanita and huckleberry, are also dwarf-sized.

Adding to the somewhat bizarre natural world of upper Jug Handle Creek, are a couple of sphagnum bogs—layers of peat standing in water— which support mosses and an insectivorous plant called sandew that uses its sticky leaves to capture its victims.

When you reach the end of Jug Handle Ecological Staircase Trail, you can join Gibney Fire Road for a quicker return to the main part of the reserve.

88

Ten Mile Beach Trail

Laguna Point to Ten Mile River: 10 miles round trip

Ten Mile Dunes and Inglenook Fen, Laguna Point and Cleone Lake. These are some of the intriguing names on an intriguing land— MacKerricher State Park. Extending from just north of the Fort Bragg city limits to Ten Mile River, this preserve offers the walker a chance to explore headlands and wetlands, sand dunes, forest and meadowland.

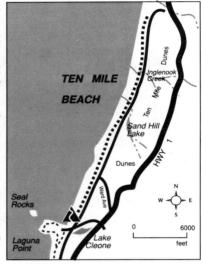

In 1868, Scottish immigrant Duncan MacKerricher paid $1.25 an acre for a former Indian reservation, El Rancho de la Laguna. MacKerricher and his heirs worked the land until 1949 when they gift-deeded it to the state.

The vast redwood forests of the coast range in the areas bordering Ten Mile River were heavily logged. An early coast railroad connected the mills of the town of Cleone with a landing at Laguna Point. Lumber was loaded onto flatcars which rolled by gravity to waiting schooners; horses hauled the cars back to the mill. At the point, the walker can see anchor pins and other signs of the old landing.

A more obvious reminder of this coast's logging history is the old haul road that crosses the park. In 1949, the road replaced a railway, which for three decades carried timber from the Ten Mile River Area to the Union Lumber Company in Fort Bragg. A 1982, winter storm washed out sections of the road, closing the five-mile stretch from Cleone Lake to Ten Mile River. The road, which today has a couple of washouts, is closed to traffic and is a superb path for walkers. (The road from Cleone Lake south to the outskirts of Fort Bragg is still open to vehicles.)

The old logging road travels the length of Ten Mile Beach to the mouth of Ten Mile River, so named because it's ten miles north of Noyo River. The beach is backed by one of the California coast's longest dune systems.

Directions to trailhead: From Highway 1, three miles north of Fort Bragg, turn west into the main entrance of MacKerricher State Park. Follow the signs to the Laguna Point Parking area.

The Walk: West of the underpass, a gravel road (as well as a steep trail) leads up to the paved ex-logging road. Walk north on the high embankment. You'll soon observe Cleone Lake, which was once a tidal lagoon before the road cut it off from the sea. Many shore and water birds visit the lake. Mill Creek, which feeds the lake, is a winter stopover for ducks and geese. Bird watchers will enjoy the mile-long walk around the lake.

Soon you'll pass some squat shore pines—a coastal form of the much-better-known ponderosa pine. You'll also walk past a side trail leading to the state park campground. A quarter-mile later another side trail beckons; this one leads over the dunes, which are covered with grasses, sand verbena and beach morning glory.

About a mile and a half north of the trailhead, you'll encounter a washed-out section of road and, a few hundred yards farther, another bad section.

Two miles north of Laguna Point, tucked in the dunes, lies Inglenook Fen. A botanist studying this unique ecosystem gave it the old English word fen—something like a bog or marsh. Sandhill Lake and the marshy area around it support many rare plants such as marsh pennywort and rein orchid, as well as many endemic varities of spiders and insects. It's a sensitive area, and not open to the public.

After walking three miles, you'll pass a couple of small creeks and begin crossing the widest part of the sand dunes, which at this point are about a mile wide and measure more than one hundred feet high. Four and a half miles from the trailhead, the road turns inland with Ten Mile River. You can continue walking north a short distance if you wish down to the mouth of Ten Mile River. It's a marsh area, inhabited by lots of ducks.

The main route travels inland above the east bank of Ten Mile River. A side trail leads southeast to a parking area beside Highway 1, while the paved road continues under the highway bridge.

▲ 89
Lost Coast Trail

Usal Beach Camp to Anderson Gulch: 5 miles round trip;
1,100-foot gain

Usal is an Indian word meaning south; it was used by 19th-century settlers to describe the Sinkyone people, who lived in a village at the mouth of what we now call Usal Creek. Usal Creek and Beach mark the southern boundary of Sinkyone Wilderness State Park, and the southern end of the magnificent Lost Coast Trail that travels the length of the park.

In 1889, J.H. Wonderly built a redwood mill, logging railway, and wharf at Usal. The operation was purchased by Captain Redwood Dollar in 1894. The property sold cheap because ship captains were quite reluctant to call at Usal; it had a reputation as one of the north coast's most dangerous doghole ports. But Captain Dollar had his own fleet, including the custom-built steam schooner Newsboy, which braved Usal landing.

Usal Mill closed in 1902, and soon burned to the ground, along with the town. No trace of the town remains. Captain Dollar went on to build a shipping empire. His Dollar Line passenger and freight vessels sailed the world.

There's a primitive state park campground located along Usal Creek near the beach. Surf fishing, beachcombing, and abalone diving attract many visitors. Good sightings of osprey diving into the surf can be enjoyed from the two-mile sand beach. A seasonal waterfall, which tumbles over the cliff edge to the beach, can be reached by walking (during a low tide) two miles upcoast.

This walk samples the Lost Coast Trail. It is not a gentle trail, and the up-and-down nature of the southern portion is typical of its entire length. Prominent ridges offer spectacular vistas of up to 100 miles of Lost Coast.

Directions to trailhead: To reach the south portion of Sinkyone Wilderness State Park at Usal Beach, take Highway 1 three miles north of the hamlet of Rockport and turn west on unsigned, unpaved County Road 431 (Usal Road). Follow this road six miles as it rises to a thousand feet, then descends to Usal Beach Camp.

Usal Road, which meanders along the north and east boundaries of the state park, is quite an adventure. The road has changed little since Jack London and his wife drove it in a horse-drawn carriage in 1911.

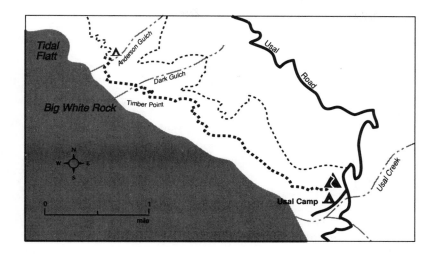

The Walk: From the signed trailhead, Lost Coast Trail rises steeply above the Usal Creek drainage. The path switchbacks through redwoods up onto a ridgeline, gentles for about two miles, then resumes climbing to a notch just below 1,320-foot high Timber Point. If you decide to call it a day here, your walk would add up to about a five-mile round trip.

From Timber Point, Lost Coast Trail descends precipitously to fern-choked Dark Gulch. The gulch was once "dark" with redwood and Douglas fir, but was heavily logged. The trail climbs out of Dark Gulch and contours on grassy slopes. As the path approaches Anderson Gulch, it swings east, then descends to a stream and a small campsite set in a meadow. There's a good view down-gulch to the sea.

▲ 90
Lost Coast Trail

Orchard Creek Camp to Bear Harbor: 3/4 mile round trip
Orchard Creek Camp to J. Smeaton Chase Grove:
4 miles round trip; 600-foot gain
Orchard Creek Camp to Wheeler Camp:
9 miles round trip; 800-foot gain

Just before the turn of the century, Bear Harbor was the scene of one of the most unusual railroad lines in history. In order to transport logs from Harvey Anderson's timber holdings, the Bear Harbor and Eel River Railroad began construction of tracks from Bear Harbor to Piercy on the Eel River. A winch lowered and raised the locomotive and cars over the first very steep stretch of narrow-gauge track near Bear Harbor. Past Usal Road, the train ran on its own power. Disaster plagued the railroad from the start. A Pacific storm destroyed Bear Harbor wharf in 1899, owner Harvey Anderson was killed in an industrial accident in 1905, and the 1906 San Francisco earthquake caused major damage to the tracks and trestles.

Today, rusted rails dangling down the cliffs at Bear Harbor, and faint traces of the railbed in Railroad Canyon, are all that remain of the railroad. (Railroad history buffs may view the steam engine used during the brief life of the Bear Harbor and Eel River Railroad at Fort Humboldt State Historic Park.) Another historical site visited by the Lost Coast Trail is the ghost town of Wheeler. Established in 1950, this company town and its modern sawmill stood for ten years. Big trucks hauled the cut lumber to Willits.

The Lost Coast Trail is interesting for more than historical reasons. In the steep canyons are stately redwood groves, standing tall above a lush understory of ferns, calypso orchids and Douglas iris. Grassy meadows are seasonally bedecked with lupine, buttercup, and Indian paintbrush. Terrific views are yours from the trail which, although it marches up and down quite a bit, never strays too far from the incessant roar of the surf.

Directions to trailhead: Follow directions for Walk #91 to Sinkyone Wilderness State Park. Stop at the park visitors center and inquire about the condition of the park road (Briceland Road or Bear Harbor Road). Except after heavy rains, most vehicles with good ground clearance can make the 2 1/2 mile distance to Bear Harbor. Beware of one nasty place—where the road crosses Flat Rock Creek. At road's end is Orchard Creek Camp and a parking area.

The Walk: Cross Orchard Creek on a small wooden bridge. The trail meanders streamside and soon passes a path lead leftward to some giant eucalyptus that shelter Railroad Creek Camp.

The path crosses Railroad Creek and joins the old railroad bed of the Bear Harbor Railroad. At one time, the tracks angled up and over the ridge to your right, and met a loading chute. Look carefully, and you'll spot some rusted rails sticking out of the clifftop.

If its low tide, pick your way over the driftwood piled up at the mouth of Railroad Creek. The guano-covered, flat-topped rock you see offshore—Morgan Rock—supported a loading pier that reached to shore.

To pick up the Lost Coast Trail, double-back from the beach a short distance. Sign the trail register located near the old corral. The path heads east up the canyon cut by Railroad Creek. Bay laurel, red alder, and maple shade the way.

The trail crosses the creek and begins climbing out of the canyon. You join an old logging road—one of several utilized by the Lost Coast Trail, as it snakes along from Bear Harbor to Usal—for a short distance. About

Lost Coast trailhead, Bear Harbor

1 1/2 miles from the trailhead, as you top a grassy ridge, you'll get a superb view of Bear Harbor and its offshore Cluster Cone rocks.

The path descends into Duffy's Gulch, which embraces a pretty stream and a redwood grove. Woodwardia and sword ferns, as well as redwood sorrel, complement the thousand- year-old redwoods. The grove is named for J. Smeaton Chase, the long-overlooked, trail rider/nature writer, whose 1913 book, "California Coastal Trails," is a classic. Chase recounts his 1912 horseback ride along the California coast from Mexico to Oregon. Quite an adventure in those days!

The trail climbs out of Duffy's Gulch and heads south along the grassy, wind-blown bluffs. By now, the astute walker is beginning to detect a pattern to the Lost Coast Trail: lots of up-and-down travel!

The route alternates between mixed conifer forest, and blue-eyed grass meadowland. A half-mile from Wheeler, you approach another redwood grove—School Marm Grove. The fern-lined trail descends with Jackass Creek to the bottom of the canyon, then over to the grassy flats where the town of Wheeler once stood.

Some cement foundations are about all that remain of the town of Wheeler. Walk past Wheeler Camp and the old town site, and follow Jackass Creek down to the beautiful black sand beach.

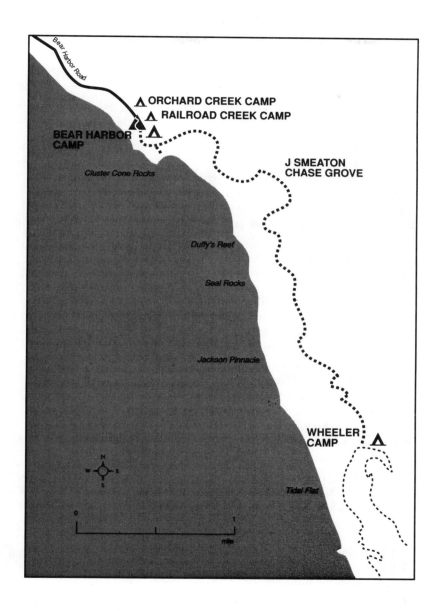

ORCHARD CREEK CAMP

RAILROAD CREEK CAMP

Bear Harbor Road

BEAR HARBOR
CAMP

Cluster Cone Rocks

J SMEATON
CHASE GROVE

Duffy's Reef

Seal Rocks

Jackson Pinnacle

WHEELER
CAMP

N
W E
S

0   1
mile

Tidal Flat

▲ 91
LOST COAST TRAIL

Needle Rock Visitors Center to Jones Beach:
2 miles round trip; 100-foot gain
Needle Rock Visitors Center to Whale Gulch:
4 1/2 miles round trip; 200-foot gain

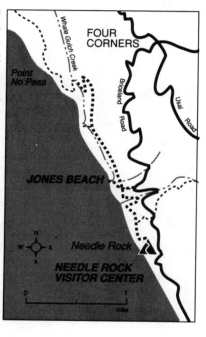

The land we now call Sinkyone Wilderness State Park has always been recognized as something special. During the late 1960s, the great Catholic theologian, Thomas Merton, felt that the Needle Rock area would be an ideal place for a life of prayer and contemplation, and talked of establishing a monastic community here.

During the 1920s, a small settlement and shipping point were established at Needle Rock. A dairy operation, complete with large stockyards, stood on the bluffs. Around the stockyards, stood a store, a hotel, school, and living quarters for the families of the dairymen. The Calvin Cooper Stewart family were the main residents of Needle Rock, and today their ranch house serves as the park visitors center.

This walk explores the northernmost, and most easily accessible, portion of the state park. It's a superb introduction to the 60-mile stretch of northern Mendocino and southern Humboldt counties known as the Lost Coast.

Directions to trailhead: From Highway 101, take either the Garberville or Redway exit and proceed to "downtown" Redway, located 3 miles north of Garberville on Business 101. Turn west on Briceland Road. After 12 miles of travel, fork left to Whitethorn. A mile or so past the hamlet of Whitethorn (Don't blink or you'll miss it), the pavement ends, and you continue on a potholed dirt/mud road for 3 1/2 more miles to a junction called

Four Corners. Leftward is Usal Road, rightward is a road climbing into the King Range National Conservation Area. Proceed straight ahead 3 1/2 miles to the Sinkyone Wilderness State Park Visitors Center. (The state park road may be impassable in winter.)

Maps and information are available at the visitors center.

The Walk: Head back up the park road toward the old barn. Notice a trail leading to the bluff edge, then down to the beach. Famed Needle Rock is a short distance up the dark sand beach.

Join the trail leading behind the barn and dipping into and out of a gully. You'll pass Barn Camp, one of the state park's environmental, or walk-in, campsites. A quarter-mile of travel brings you to Streamside Camp, another of the park's primitive, but superb, camps.

You'll soon reach a junction with a trail climbing to the east. This is Low Gap Trail, which ascends the coastal bluffs and crosses the park road. The trail plunges into the forest, travels along Low Gap Creek, and, after a stiff climb, reaches Usal Road and Low Gap Camp.

Lost Coast Trail, your route, continues along the lovely bluffs to Low Gap Creek, heads inland briefly, then crosses a bridge over the creek. The path heads toward a stand of eucalyptus, which shelters the Jones Beach campsites.

The trail forks. The left fork leads a quarter-mile to Jones Beach. If it's low tide, you can walk back to the trailhead on the beach.

Lost Coast Trail proceeds with the right fork and soon descends into a canyon. You cross two creeks, which drain an area that can be very marshy during the rainy season. You walk near the edge of a cattail-lined pond, climb to higher ground, and pass a second pond.

Soon you are treated to a bird's-eye-view of Whale Gulch. At the mouth of Whale Gulch is a small lagoon, and piles of driftwood logs. The trail descends into the gulch. A newly-constructed section of the Lost Coast Trail travels inland along the south wall of Whale Gulch. Eventually, this trail crosses the gulch, and heads up Chemise Mountain to join the trail system in the King Range National Conservation Area.

 **92**

Chemise Mountain Trail

Wailaki Recreation Site to Chemise Mountain:
3 miles round trip; 750-foot gain
Wailaki Recreation Site to Beach:
9 miles round trip; 3,000-foot loss and gain

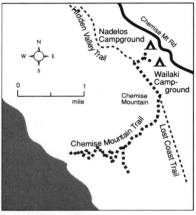

Chemise Mountain Trail explores the southern section of the 60,000-acre King Range National Conservation Area. The path ascends Chemise Mountain for a dramatic view of the Lost Coast. The trail connects to Lost Coast Trail, which leads to the Whale Gulch area of Sinkyone Wilderness State Park. Chemise Mountain Trail also makes a precipitous 3,000-foot descent to an isolated beach; however, the last quarter-mile of this trail is subject to landslides and is not recommended for travel. Seasoned hikers should check on the latest trail conditions with BLM's Arcata or Ukiah offices.

A walk along Chemise Mountain Trail offers the walker the full drama of the King Range. The mountains seem to rise straight out of the surf; in fact, these are the steepest coastal mountains in California. The view from Chemise Mountain on a fogless spring day is unforgettable, as is the return climb from the beach. The optional trek toward the beach—and the 3,000-foot climb back to the trailhead—is the most difficult walk described in this book.

Directions to trailhead: Exit Highway 101 in Garberville and proceed 2 1/2 miles north on Business 101 to Redway. Turn left on Briceland Road and continue past the hamlet of Briceland. Veer right on Shelter Cove Road, and continue up and over a ridgeline to Bear Creek drainage, where you'll fork left on Chemise Mountain Road. Park at Wailaki Recreation Site.

The Walk: The path crosses a bridge over Bear Creek and passes a junction with the King Range Nature Trail. (The nature trail meanders with Bear Creek through examples of native flora, particularly within the redwood community.) Most of the trees in the King Range are Douglas fir, as you'll soon notice when you begin ascending Chemise Mountain.

A quarter-mile ascent brings you to a junction with a trail, popular with horsemen, that leads from Nadelos Campground. Switchbacking along toward the top of a ridge, you pass another trail—Hidden Valley Trail, which forks right.

As you angle along the ridgetop, you lose the Douglas fir and enter a hardwood forest. When you first gain the ridgetop, your view is blocked by chaparral. Keep going to a clear area and a sign soon directs you to the very top of 2,596-foot Chemise Mountain.

The panorama is impressive, particularly to the south, where you have a great view of Sinkyone Wilderness State Park. King's Peak is the dominant promontory to the north. Far below, is Shelter Cove.

Whale Gulch is immediately to the south. On a clear day, the many sharp ridges and steep canyons of the state park's coastline are visible. Sometimes you can count 8, 10, or even a dozen ridges—meaning, of course, that walking the Lost Coast Trail through the park is quite a rugged adventure.

Scars from the 1973 Finley Creek Fire are evident near the summit of Chemise Mountain. Chemise, or greasewood burns very hot, and is a curse to firefighters, because the plant is full of oil and nearly explodes when afire.

From the summit, you follow a now rather overgrown firebreak a few hundred feet to the signed trail leading to the beach. The path meanders through a burn area and descends past a stand of knobcone pine. A half-mile's travel brings you to a ridge, located south of Chemise Creek. You follow this ridge oceanward. Emerging from hardwood forest, the route joins a fuel break for a short distance, then descends steeply down a Douglas fir-dotted slope.

Two miles from the peak, you arrive at a meadow, perched a thousand feet above the ocean. Flat ground is scarce in these parts, so this might be the opportune place to rest, or to eat your lunch. A side trail branches due south; it leads to another, larger meadow.

Chemise Mountain Trail switchbacks down the precipitous slopes. You'll pass through a dark, spooky forest of old growth Douglas fir. A quarter-mile from the beach, you reach the portion of the path ruined by landslides.

You must return the way you came. The lovely, one-mile long beach is backed by two impassable points—both called Point No Pass. The northern point can be rounded at minus tides, but it's risky business and not recommended.

93
King Crest Trail

South Trailhead (Saddle Mt. Rd.) to Kings Peak:
5 miles round trip;1,000-foot gain

The King Range seems to rise straight from the sea; this abrupt rise is unsurpassed on California's coast, and is found in few places in the world. Kings Peak, at 4,087 feet the highest summit in the range, is less than three miles from the ocean.

The King Range is one of the most geologically-active mountain ranges in America. The North American plate grinds over the Pacific plate, fracturing the bedrock as the mountains lift skyward. Scientists believe that tectonic movement has caused the shoreline to lift more than sixty feet over the last 6,000 years.

King Crest Trail stretches about eight miles over the dramatic ridgetops of the King Range. This walk explores the geologically-fascinating signature peak of the King Range, and offers grand views of the conservation area.

Directions to trailhead: From Redway, take Briceland Road past the hamlet of Briceland. Veer right on Shelter Cove Road, which ascends a 2,000-foot pass. Shelter Cove Road descends to Shelter Cove, but you turn right on Horse Mountain Road and proceed seven miles. Just before Horse Mountain Recreation Site, turn left on Saddle Mountain Road, which you'll follow seven miles to signed King Crest trailhead.

The Walk: You'll find a hiker's sign-in register a hundred yards up the trail. The narrow trail leads along the sharp spine of the ridge, which has a particularly dramatic fall-off on the west side. You travel through a madrone forest and tackle some fairly steep switchbacks.

As you walk through an area of low-lying brush, you'll get your first view of Kings Peak, companion sharp ridges, and off in the distance, North Side Peak. You might be peeling off sweaters and jackets on this next stretch of

240

trail; there's about a 20 degree difference in temperature between the cool tanoak and madrone woodland and the exposed ridgetop.

At a signed junction, the trail's right fork leads to Maple Camp, which has water—a consideration if you're planning a long hike or backpack on King Crest Trail. A half-mile's ascent on the trail's left fork brings you to Kings Peak. On a clear day, you'll see Mattole Valley and grassy Cooksie Ridge and Spanish Ridge. To the east is the Eel River drainage and the peaks of the Yolla Bolly Wilderness. To the south is Sinkyone Wilderness State Park. To the west lie the canyons cut by the various forks of Big Flat Creek, as well as the wide blue Pacific.

Twenty-five miles of rugged Lost Coast are protected by King Range National Conservation Area

94
Lost Coast Trail

Mattole River to Punta Gorda Lighthouse: 6 miles round trip

The Mattole River marks the northern boundary of the Bureau of Land Management's King Range National Conservation Area. From the trailhead at Mouth of Mattole Recreation Site, the Lost Coast Trail travels 24 miles along the beach to Shelter Cove. Shipwrecks, a variety of marine life, and magnificent black sand beaches are some of the attractions of what many walkers consider the wildest coastline in California.

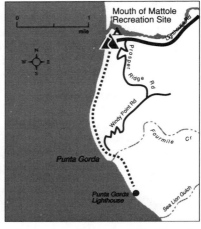

The sleepy, storybook hamlet of Petrolia, located near the river mouth, was the site of the state's first producing oil wells, drilled here in 1865. Leland Stanford's Mattole Petroleum Company had the most successful well—Union Well— which produced a hundred barrels of oil at a one barrel a day pace.

After the oil boom ended, settlers came to the Mattole Valley to take advantage of the fertile farmland and rich pasture. Mattole Valley is one of the wettest places on the Pacific Coast. The town of Honeydew, immediately to the north of the King Range, records an average of more than a hundred inches of rain a year. During extremely wet years, more than two hundred inches of rain may fall on the Lost Coast.

Adjacent grazing and logging have unfortunately taken their toll on the Mattole River. As heavy rains washed the denuded hillsides to the sea, millions of cubic yards of rock and gravel were dumped into the Mattole. Gravel bars formed, which altered the course of the river. Time and nature are slowly healing the Mattole, but the river will continue to meander off-course for many more years.

California's best beach backpacking trip is the trek from the mouth of the Mattole to Shelter Cove. A more moderate journey of three miles along the Lost Coast Trail takes the walker to the abandoned Coast Guard Lighthouse at Punta Gorda.

In 1911, after several ships were wrecked on the rocks and reefs off the King Range Coast, a lighthouse was built a mile south of Punta Gorda—whose name means "massive point." The lighthouse, which shined its warning beacon for four decades, shut down in 1951 due to high maintenance costs.

Directions to trailhead: From Highway 101 in Fortuna, take the Ferndale exit and follow the signs to Petrolia. Turn west on Lighthouse Road, following it five miles to its end at the Mouth of the Mattole Recreation Site.

The Walk: Before heading south, walk a quarter-mile north to the mouth of the river. Sea gulls and ospreys circle overhead. Harbor seals frequent the tidal area where the Mattole meets the Pacific.

Walk south along the wild coast. The low dunes back of the beach are dotted in spring with sea rocket and sand verbena. Thin waterfalls cascade over the steep cliffs to the beach.

Two miles from the trailhead, you'll round Punta Gorda, which serves as a rookery for the Steller's sea lion. A mile south of the point is the old Punta Gorda Lighthouse. Beyond is another twenty miles of beach, the wildest in California.

Punta Gorda Lighthouse

95
Rim Trail

Palmer's Point to Agate Beach Campground: 4 miles round trip

Though Patrick's Point State Park is positioned in the heart of the redwoods, other trees—Sitka spruce, Douglas fir, and red alder—predominate on the park's rocky promontories. The state park takes its name from Patrick Beegan, who homesteaded this dramatic, densely forested headland in 1851.

For hundreds of years Yurok Indians spent their summers in the Abalone Point area of the headlands. The Yurok gathered shellfish and hunted sea lions. Game and a multitude of berries were plentiful in the surrounding forest. The area now called Patrick's Point also had some spiritual significance to the Indians. According to the Yurok, Sumig, spirit of the porpoises, retired to Patrick's Point when humans began populating the world.

Rim Trail follows an old Indian pathway over the park's bluffs. Spur trails lead to rocky points that jut into the Pacific and offer commanding views of Trinidad Head to the south and Big Lagoon to the north.

Directions to trailhead: Patrick's Point State Park is located thirty miles north of Eureka and five miles north of Trinidad. Exit Highway 101 on Patrick's Point Drive and follow this road to the park. Once past the park entrance station, follow the signs to Palmer Point.

The Walk: The trail plunges into a lush community of ferns, salmonberry and salal. The scolding krrrack-krrrack of the Steller jay is the only note of dissent heard along the trail.

Abalone Point is the first of a half-dozen spur trails that lead from Rim Trail to Rocky Point, Mussel Rocks, Patrick's Point, Wedding Rock and Agate Beach. Take any or all of them. (These side trails can sometimes be confused with Rim Trail; generally speaking, the spurs are much more steep than the Rim Trail, which contours along without much elevation change.)

From Patrick's Point and the other promontories, admire the precipitous cliffs and rock-walled inlets. Gaze offshore at the sea stacks, a line of soldiers battered by the surging sea. Seals and sea lions haul out on the offshore rocks, which also double as rookeries for gulls, cormorants and pigeon guillemots.

Rim Trail meanders through a tapestry of trillium and moss, rhododendron and azalea. Sword ferns point the way to a grove of red alder.

Rim Trail ends at the north loop of the Agate Beach Campground road.

Those walkers wishing to explore Agate Beach should continue a short distance along the road to the signed trailhead for Agate Beach Trail. This short, but very steep, trail switchbacks down to the beach.

In marked contrast to the park's rocky shore that you observed from the Rim Trail, Agate Beach is a wide swath of dark sand stretching north to the state parks at Big Lagoon.

Beachcombers prospect for agates in the gravel bars and right at the surf line. The agates found here are a nearly transparent variety of quartz, polished by sand and the restless sea. Jade, jaspar and other semi-precious stones are sometimes found here. One more noteworthy sight is the huge quantity and unique sea-sculpted quality of the driftwood on this beach.

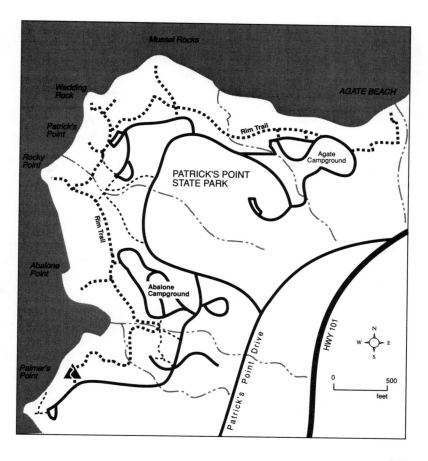

96
Redwood Creek Trail

Redwood Creek Trailhead to Tall Trees Grove:
8 1/4 miles one way; 500 foot gain

Redwood Creek Trail travels through the heart of Redwood National Park to Tall Trees Grove, site of the world's tallest tree. After one of the 1960s' classic conservation battles, a narrow corridor of land along Redwood Creek was acquired to protect the world's highest tree, a coast redwood measuring 367.8 feet. This giant was discovered in 1963 by a National Geographic expedition.

The nine-mile stretch along Redwood Creek known as "the worm" was downslope from private timberlands, where there was extensive and insensitive clear cut logging. Resulting slope erosion and stream sediments threatened the big trees, so to protect this watershed, the National Park Service purchased an additional 48,000 acres, mostly in Redwood Creek basin. For more than a decade, the park service has been rehabilitating scarred slopes, and planting Douglas fir and redwood.

Redwood Creek Trail follows an abandoned logging road on a gentle ascent from the outskirts of Orick to Tall Trees Grove. The trail stays above and just out of sight of Redwood Creek.

Summer visitors can take advantage of a shuttle bus service that runs from the Redwood Information Center and the Redwood Creek Trailhead to Tall Trees Grove. From the Tall Trees, walkers may follow Redwood Creek Trail back to their vehicle, parked at the trailhead. For more information, call (707) 488-3461.

One word of caution: The three bridges that cross Redwood Creek are in place only during the summer. Use your best judgement in deciding whether or not to attempt this hike during the wetter seasons.

Directions to trailhead: From Highway 101, about 2 miles north of the Redwood National Park Visitors Center and the town of Orick, turn east on Bald Hills Road. Take the first right turn to the Redwood Creek trailhead.

The Walk: The first 1 1/2 miles of trail, from the trailhead to the first bridge crossing of Redwood Creek, passes through regenerating forest, as well as old growth Sitka spruce and redwood. The trail also passes a meadowland that flanks the river.

Occasional clearings and the bridge crossings allow the walker to get the "big picture" of Redwood Creek. Three distinct communities of flora can

be discerned: Extensive grass prairie, emerald green during the wet season and golden brown during drier months, dominates the eastern slopes above Redwood Creek. Downslope of the grassland are vast clearcuts—ugly and slow to heal. Near the creek are the groves of old growth redwood and a lush understory of salmonberry, oxalis and sword fern.

During the summer months, the walker may descend to Redwood Creek and travel the creek's gravel bars nearly to the Tall Trees Grove. The river bars are fine pathways and also serve as campsites for backpackers.

Continue through the forest primeval. The redwoods congregate in especially large families on the alluvial flats along the stream.

Enjoy the loop trail through the Tall Trees Grove before taking the Tall Trees Trail up to C-Line Road, where the shuttle bus stops.

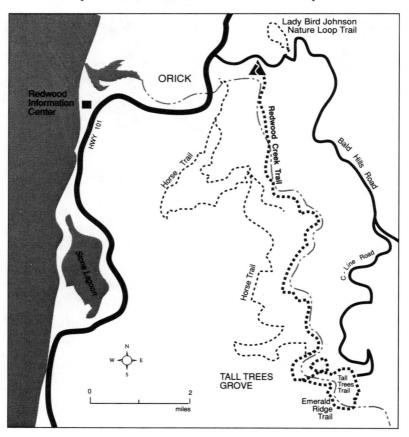

▲ 97
Gold Bluffs Trail

Loop through Fern Canyon: 3/4-mile round trip
Fern Canyon-Gold Bluffs-Gold Bluffs Beach:
5 miles round trip; 500-foot gain

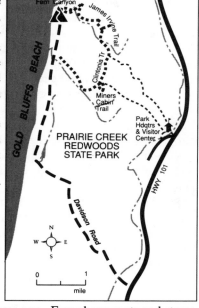

The redwoods seem most at home on Gold Bluffs. Dim and quiet, wrapped in mist and silence, the redwoods roof a moist and mysterious world. Prairie Creek Redwoods State Park trails meander over lush ground and the walker's lungs are filled with the fragrance of wood and water.

Many beautiful "fern canyons" are found along the North Coast, but this Fern Canyon is undoubtedly the most awe-inspiring. Bracken, five-finger, lady, sword, and chain ferns smother the precipitous walls of the canyon. Bright yellow monkeyflowers abound, as well as fairy lanterns, those creamy white, or greenish, bell-shaped flowers that hang in clusters.

Ferns are descendants of an ancient group of plants which were much more numerous 200 million years ago. Ferns have roots and stems similar to flowering plants, but are considered to be a primitive form of plant life because they reproduce by spores, not seeds.

Gold Bluffs was named in 1850 when prospectors found some gold flakes in the beach sand. The discovery caused a minor "gold rush." A tent city sprang up on the beach but litle gold was taken.

This walk explores some of the highlights of Prairie Creek Redwoods State Park—Fern Canyon, magnificent redwood groves, and Gold Bluffs Beach.

Directions to trailhead: From Highway 101, six miles north of Orick, turn west on Davison Road. The dirt, washboard road descends logged slopes and through second-growth redwoods to the beach. The road heads north along Gold Bluffs Beach. One and a half miles past the campground, the road deadends at the Fern Canyon Trailhead.

The Walk: The path leads along the pebbled floor of Fern Canyon. In the wettest places, the route follows wooden planks across Home Creek. With sword and five-finger ferns pointing the way, you pass through marshy areas covered with swamp grass and dotted with skunk cabbage. Lurking about are Pacific giant salamanders.

A half-mile from the trailhead, the path climbs out of the canyon to intersect James Irvine Trail, named for a man who contributed much to the formation of the redwood parks.

The Irvine Trail crosses to the south side of the canyon and proceeds southeast with Home Creek.

The trail reaches the upper neck of Fern Canyon and junctions with Clintonia Trail. (James Irvine Trail continues ascending through dense redwood forest to a trailhead near the park visitors center.) Clintonia Trail leads a mile through virgin redwood groves to a junction with Miners Ridge Trail. Bear right.

Part of Miners Ridge Trail is an old logging road, used by mule-drawn wagons. The trail was also a pack train route for the Gold Bluffs miners. You'll pass an intersection with Miner's Cabin Trail and descend with Squashan Creek to the sea.

Gold Bluffs Beach is a beauty—eleven miles of wild, driftwood-littered shore, backed by extensive dunes. Sand verbena, bush lupine, and wild strawberry splash color on the sand. It's a one mile beachcomb back to the trailhead.

Lucky walkers might catch a glimpse of the herd of Roosevelt elk that roam the park. These graceful animals look like a cross between a South American llama and a deer and convince walkers that they have indeed entered an enchanted land.

Roosevelt elk roam Prairie Creek Redwood State Park

 **98**

Coastal Trail

Lagoon Creek Fishing Access to Hidden Beach: 2 miles round trip
Lagoon Creek Fishing Access to Requa Overlook: 8 miles roundtrip;
        200-foot gain

The partially completed Coastal Trail—or Redwood Coastal Trail as national park rangers often refer to it—is a 40-mile pathway that connects state and national parklands.

One of the more spectacular sections of the trail is the four miles between Lagoon Creek and the mouth of the Klamath River.

Lagoon Creek empties into a manmade pond, formed in 1940 when the lumber mill here dammed the creek to form a log pond. The creek and pond became part of Redwood National Park in 1972. Heart-shaped yellow pond lilies float in the tranquil pond, which is habitat for ducks, egrets, herons, and red-winged blackbirds.

Adding to the pleasure of a walk in this area is the Yurok Loop Nature Trail which explores the lagoon area. The walker may use one-half the loop on departure and the second half on the return trip. Interpretive brochures are (sometimes) available at the parking area.

Directions to trailhead: Lagoon Creek Fishing Access is located just west of Highway 101, five miles north of the town of Klamath.

The Walk: Head south along the Yurok Loop Nature Trail, which travels through a dense canopy of oak, alder and willow. From the blufftop are occasional views of the beaches below.

Coastal Trail veers right from the nature trail and follows a fern-lined path to a grove of red alder. During spring and summer, hikers may observe hummingbirds extracting nectar from pink-flowered salmon-berry bushes.

About a mile from the trailhead is Hidden Beach, a driftwood-piled sandy beach that's ideal for a picnic.

From Hidden Beach, the trail ascends into Sitka spruce forest. Halfway to Requa Overlook, Coastal Trail crests a divide and continues on through thick forest. A few overlooks allow the walker glimpses of the bold headlands north and south, and of the wave-cut terraces below. Sea lions and seals may haul out on offshore rocks.

Coastal Trail bears southeast to Requa Overlook, which offers picnic sites and striking views of the mouth of the Klamath River. The overlook is also a good place to watch for migrating California gray whales.

▲ 99

Damnation Creek Trail

Highway 101 to Damnation Cove: 5 miles round trip;
900-foot loss and gain

Steep Damnation Creek Trail plunges through a virgin redwood forest to a hidden rocky beach. Giant ferns, and the pink and purple rhododendron blossoms climbing thirty feet overhead, contribute to the impression that one has strayed into a tropical rain forest.

The creek name, as the story goes, was proffered by early settlers who had a devil of a time making their way through the thick forest near the creek banks. Even trailblazer Jedediah Smith, whose expedition camped alongside Damnation Creek in June of 1828, found it very rough going.

Yurok Indians used the trail along Damnation Creek to reach the beach, where they gathered seaweed and shellfish.

Allow extra time for this walk; it's a strenuous journey back to the highway from Damnation Cove.

Directions to trailhead: Park at the Henry Solon Grove Memorial turnout (located at mileage marker 16), just off Highway 101, about 4 miles south of the Del Norte Redwoods State Park campground entrance.

The Walk: The trail climbs through redwood forest for a quarter-mile, crests a ridge and begins its oceanward descent. Joining the redwoods on the wet and wild coastal slope are other big trees—Sitka spruce and Douglas fir—and a carpet of oxalis.

About halfway to the beach, the walker is treated to tree-framed views of the Pacific as the trail angles along with Damnation Creek. You'll cross a paved road—old Highway 101. Rocky Damnation Cove is best explored at low tide when you can view the tidepools.

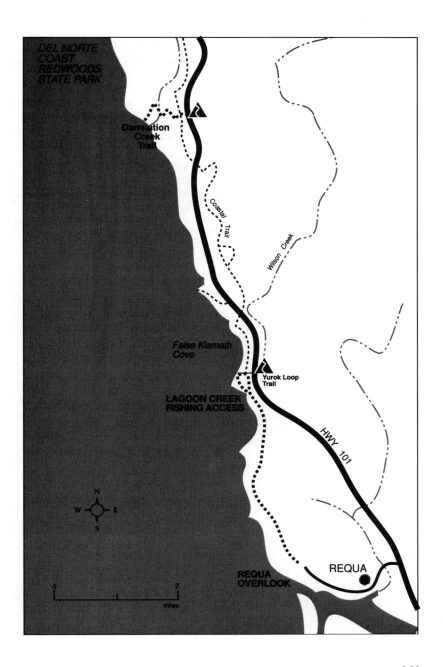

DEL NORTE
COAST
REDWOODS
STATE PARK

Damnation
Creek
Trail

Coastal Trail

Wilson Creek

False Klamath
Cove

Yurok Loop
Trail

LAGOON CREEK
FISHING ACCESS

HWY 101

N
W E
S

0 2
miles

REQUA
OVERLOOK

REQUA

 **100**

Pelican Bay Trail

Radio Road to Point St. George: 2 miles round trip
Radio Road to Lake Talawa: 8 miles round trip

Extending between Pyramid Point at the mouth of the Smith River south to Point St. George, Pelican Bay is one of California's most bountiful fisheries. Salmon, rockfish and sole are caught offshore, while the Dungeness crab is taken along the coast.

Attracted by the ocean's abundant harvest, Tolowa Indians camped in the Pelican Bay area as early as 300 B.C.. The Tolowa fished salmon from the Smith River mouth, gathered mussels and clams, and hunted sea lions.

Two coastal lagoons—Lakes Earl and Talawa—are separated from the bay by a sandbar. The mostly freshwater Lake Earl and the more saline Lake Talawa host more than 250 species of birds. The lakes are a crucial stopover for birds traveling the Pacific Flyway, the west coast bird migration route. Sometimes as many as one hundred thousand birds can be sighted here. Surrounding the lakes are saltwater marshland and freshwater wetlands, as well as far-reaching sand dunes.

Point St. George on the south end of Pelican Bay is a dramatic headland, at the foot of which are rich tidepools. Extending west of the point is St. George Reef, which includes Seal Rocks, a seal and sea lion rookery. At the end of the reef, some seven miles from the mainland, stands St. George Lighthouse, abandoned in 1975 due to extrordinarily high maintenance costs. The lighthouse was built in 1892, in tardy response to the 1865 wreck of the Pacific Mail steamer Brother Jonathan, a tragedy that claimed the lives of 213 passengers. Crescent City's Brother Jonathan Park has a cemetery and memorial honoring those who perished.

This walk offers two different ways to explore Pelican Bay. A walk south takes you to the rich tidepool area of Point St. George while beach walking north leads to Lakes Earl and Talawa.

Directions to trailhead: From Highway 101 just north of Crescent City, exit on Washington Boulevard and drive west. Washington becomes Radio Road, which you follow to its terminus at a parking area.

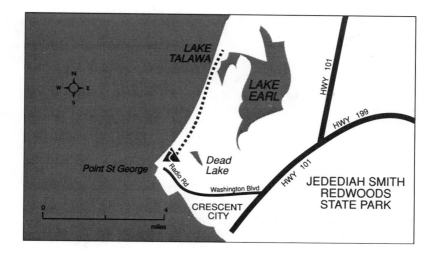

The Walk: From the parking lot of a former Coast Guard Station, follow the trail a hundred yards down grass-covered hillocks toward the shore. Head south to reach the Point St. George tidepools.

The crashing sea has gouged pockets into the sandstone and shale point. The unusually rich tidepools, fringed with kelp and sea palms, are filled with a myriad of life. Walkers may stalk the amazing 24-armed sunflower starfish, one of the largest (2 feet across) and fastest stars found on the California coast.

The journey northward from the trailhead takes you along a beach backed by dunes. About a half-mile inland is Dead Lake, a small freshwater lake that, like so many bodies of water along the redwood coast, was formerly a lumber mill pond. The lake, now state park property, is habitat for wood ducks.

Continue along the driftwood littered beach to Lake Talawa, which is surrounded by a marshland. Opportunities for exploration of Lake Talawa and its larger neighbor, Lake Earl, are limited by the marshy terrain and mudflats, which are better suited to the needs of soft-shelled clams than walkers. After observing the multitude of waterfowl, including canvasbacks and the endangered Aleutian goose, return along the beach to the trailhead.

Information Sources

Andrew Molera State Park
c/o Pfeiffer Big Sur State Park
Big Sur, CA 93920
(408) 667-2316

Angel Island State Park
P.O. Box 318
Tiburon, CA 94920
(415) 435-1915

Ano Nuevo State Reserve
New Years Creek Road
Pescadero, CA 94060
(415) 879-0227

Big Basin Redwoods State Park
21600 Big Basin Way
Boulder Creek, CA 95006
(408) 338-6132

Border Field State Park
c/o Frontera District
3990 Old Town Ave. #300-C
San Diego, CA 92110
(619) 428-3034

Butano State Park
P.O. Box 9
Pescadero, CA 94060
(415) 879-0173

Cabrillo Marine Museum
3720 Stephen M. White Dr.
San Pedro, CA 90731
(213) 548-7561

Cabrillo National Monument
P.O. Box 6670
San Diego, CA 92106
(619) 293-5450

California Coastal Commission
631 Howard Street, 4th Floor
San Francisco, CA 94105
(415) 543-8555

**California Dept. of Parks
& Recreation**
P.O. Box 942896
Sacramento, CA 94296
(916) 445-6477

Catalina Island
Avalon Chamber of Commerce:
(213) 510-1520
L.A. Co. Dept. Parks & Rec.:
(213) 510-0688

Channel Islands National Park
1901 Spinnaker Drive
Ventura, CA 93001
(805) 644-8157

China Camp State Park
East San Pedro Road
San Rafael, CA 94901
(415) 456-1286/456-0766

Crystal Cove State Park
18331 Enterprise Lane
Huntington Beach, CA 92648
(714) 494-3539

**Del Norte Coast Redwoods
State Park**
P.O. Drawer J
Crescent City, CA 95531
(707) 464-9533

**Forest of Nisene Marks
State Park**
c/o Santa Cruz Mountains District
101 N. Big Trees Park Road
Felton, CA 95018
(408) 335-4598/335-9106

Fort Ross State Historic Park
19005 Coast Hwy. 1
Jenner, CA 95460
(707) 847-3286

Garrapata State Park
c/o Pfeiffer Big Sur State Park
Big Sur, CA 93920
(408) 667-2316

Gaviota State Park
#10 Refugio Beach Rd.
Goleta, CA 93117
(805) 968-0019

**Golden Gate National
Recreation Area**
Fort Mason, Building 201
San Francisco, CA 94123
(415) 556-0560

Gualala Point Regional Park
Sonoma County Regional Parks
2403 Professional Drive, Suite 100
Santa Rosa, CA 95401
(707) 785-2377/527-2041

**Hearst San Simeon
State Historical Monument**
P.O. Box 8
San Simeon, CA 93452
(805) 927-4621

**Henry Cowell Redwoods
State Park**
101 N. Big Trees Park Road
Felton, CA 95018
(408) 335-4598

Jalama Beach County Park
(805) 736-6316

**Jedediah Smith Redwoods
State Park**
4241 Kings Valley Road
Crescent City, CA 95531
(707) 464-9533/458-3310

**King Range National
Conservation Area**
U.S. Bureau of Land Management
Arcata Resource Area
P.O. Box 1112
Arcata, CA 95521
(707) 822-7648

Leo Carrillo State Beach
35000 Pacific Coast Highway
Malibu, CA 90265
(818) 706-1310

Los Padres National Forest
6144 Calle Real
Goleta, CA 93117
(805) 683-6711

MacKerricher State Park
c/o Mendocino District
P.O. Box 440
Mendocino, CA 95460
(707) 964-9112/937-5804

Malibu Creek State Park
28754 Mulholland Hwy.
Agoura, CA 91301
(818) 706-1310

McGrath State Beach
c/o Channel Coast District
24 E. Main Street
Ventura, CA 93001
(805) 483-8034/654-4611

**Mendocino Headlands
State Park**
P.O. Box 440
Mendocino, CA 95460
(707) 937-5804

Montana de Oro State Park
c/o Morro Bay State Park
Morro Bay, CA 93442
(805) 772-2560/772-8812

Monterey Bay Aquarium
886 Cannery Row
Monterey, CA 93940
(408) 375-3333

Monterey State Historic Park
#20 Custom House Plaza
Monterey, CA 93940
(408) 649-2836

Morro Bay State Park
Morro Bay, CA 93442
(805) 772-2560

Mount Tamalpais State Park
801 Panoramic Highway
Mill Valley, CA 94941
(415) 388-2070

Patrick's Point State Park
Trinidad, CA 95570
(707) 677-3570

Pismo Dunes State Beach
Pier Avenue
Oceano, CA 93445
(805) 489-2684

Point Lobos State Reserve
c/o Monterey District
#20 Custom House Plaza
Monterey, CA 93940
(408) 624-4909

Point Mugu State Park
c/o Santa Monica Mtns. District
2860-A Camino Dos Rios
Newbury Park, CA 91320
(818) 706-1310/(805) 987-3303

Point Reyes National Seashore
Bear Valley Road
Point Reyes, CA 94956
(415) 663-1092

Point Sal State Beach
c/o La Purisima Mission SHP
RRFD 102
Lompoc, CA 93436
(805) 733-3713

Point Sur Lightstation
(408) 667-2316

Prairie Creek Redwoods State Park
Orick, CA 95555
(707) 488-2171

258

Redwood National Park
1111 2nd Street
Crescent City, CA 95531
(707) 464-6101

Russian Gulch State Park
P.O. Box 440
Mendocino, CA 95460
(707) 937-5804

Salt Point State Park
25050 Coast Hwy. 1
Jenner, CA 95450
(707) 865-2391

**Santa Monica Mountains
National Recreation Area**
22900 Ventura Blvd., Suite 140
Woodland Hills, CA 91364
(818) 888-3770

**Scripps Institution of
Oceanography**
Aquarium and Museum
8602 La Jolla Shores Drive
La Jolla, CA 92093
(619) 534-4086

Silver Strand State Beach
5000 Hwy. 75
Coronado, CA 92118
(619) 435-5184

Sinkyone Wilderness State Park
P.O. Box 245
Whitethorn, CA 95489
(707) 986-7711

Sonoma Coast State Beaches
Bodega Bay, CA 94923
(707) 875-3483

State Coastal Conservancy
1330 Broadway, Suite 1100
Oakland, CA 94612
(415) 464-1015

Tomales Bay State Park
Star Route
Inverness, CA 94937
(415) 669-1140

Topanga State Park
20825 Entrada Road
Topanga, CA 90290
(213) 455-2465

Torrey Pines State Reserve
c/o San Diego Coast District
2680 Carlsbad Blvd.
Carlsbad, CA 92008
(619) 755-2063

Van Damme State Park
P.O. Box 440
Mendocino, CA 95460
(707) 937-0851/937-5804

INDEX

Coastal Organizations

American Oceans Campaign
2219 Main Street #2-B
Santa Monica, CA 90405

**Californians Organized to
Acquire Access to State Tidelands**
P.O. Box 3284
Santa Rosa, CA 95402

Center for Marine Conservation
312 Sutter Street, Suite 316
San Francisco, CA 94108
(415) 391-6204

Central Coast Conservation Center
725 Main Street
Half Moon Bay, CA 94019
(415) 726-3613

Central Coast Regional Studies Program
116 New Montgomery Street #910
San Francisco, CA 94105
(415) 243-8003

Coastal Concern
GGNRA Building #1055
Sausalito, CA 94965
(415) 381-5499

Coastwalk
2126 Orchard Street
Santa Rosa, CA 95404
(707) 545-0189

Citizens for a Better Environment
942 Market Street #505
San Francisco, CA 94102
(415) 788-0690

**Environmental Health Coalition
(Clean Bay Campaign)**
1844 Third Avenue
San Diego, CA 92101
(619) 235-0281

Greenpeace
Fort Mason Building E
San Francisco, CA 94123
(415) 474-6767

Heal the Bay
1650 10th Street #A
Santa Monica, CA 90404
(213) 399-1146

League for Coastal Protection
P.O. Box 421698
San Francisco, CA 94142

Mendocino Environmental Center
106 W. Standley Street
Ukiah, CA 95482
(707) 468-1660

**Mendocino Ocean Protection
Coalition**
P.O. Box 498
Mendocino, CA 95460
(707) 937-0700

**Pacific Coast Federation of
Fishermens Association**
P.O. Box 989
Sausalito, CA 94966
(415) 332-5080

Save Our Shores
P.O. Box 1560
Santa Cruz, CA 95061
(408) 425-1769

Save San Francisco Bay Association
P.O. Box 925
Berkeley, CA 94701
(415) 849-3044

Sea Shepherd Conservation Society
P.O. Box 7000-S
Redondo Beach, CA 90277
(213) 373-6979

Surf Rider Foundation
P.O. Box 2704 #86
Huntington Beach, CA 92647
(714) 960-8390

Great Guides
to the Great Outdoors
from Olympus Press

- *California State Parks Guide*

- *Coast Walks: One Hundred Adventures Along the California Coast*

- *Day Hiker's Guide to Southern California*

- *Day Hiker's Guide to Southern California Volume II*

- *East Mojave Desert: A Visitor's Guide*